ReadSmart 1
HIGH BEGINNING

Cheryl Pavlik

McGraw-Hill ESL/ELT

ReadSmart 1

Published by McGraw-Hill ESL/ELT, a business unit of The McGraw-Hill Companies, Inc. 1221 Avenue of the Americas, New York, NY 10020. Copyright © 2004 by The McGraw-Hill Companies, Inc. All rights reserved. No part of this publication may be reproduced or distributed in any form or by any means, or stored in a database or retrieval system, without the prior written consent of The McGraw-Hill Companies, Inc., including, but not limited to, in any network or other electronic storage or transmission, or broadcast for distance learning.

This book is printed on recycled, acid-free paper containing 10% post-consumer waste.

1 2 3 4 5 6 7 8 9 QPD 9 8 7 6 5 4

ISBN: 0-07-283891-4

Editorial director: *Tina B. Carver*
Senior sponsoring editor: *Thomas Healy*
Developmental editors: *Susan Johnson, Annie Sullivan*
Production managers: *Juanita Thompson, MaryRose Bollwage*
Editorial assistant: *Kasey Williamson*
Cover designer: *Martini Graphic Services, Inc.*
Interior designer: *Acento Visual*
Art: *Martini Graphic Services, Inc.*
Photo credits: p 36, © *Bettmann/CORBIS;* p 43, © *Royalty-free, Digital Vision;* p 58, © *Robert Holmes/CORBIS;* p 93, © *Richard T. Nowitz/CORBIS;* p 111, © *Royalty-Free/CORBIS;* p 123, *We apologize for any apparent infringement of copyright and if notified, the publisher will be pleased to rectify any errors of omissions at the earliest opportunity;* p 165, © *Earl & Nazima Kowall/CORBIS;* p 179, © *David Samuel Robbins/CORBIS;* p 184, © *John Springer Collection/CORBIS;* p 196, © *Bettmann/CORBIS;* p 197, © *Bettmann/CORBIS;* p 201, © *Robert Essel NYC/CORBIS;* p 203, © *Mark E. Gibson/CORBIS;* p 214, © *Bettmann/CORBIS*

McGraw-Hill ESL/ELT

ReadSmart 1
HIGH BEGINNING

Table of Contents

Acknowledgements   viii
To the Teacher   viii

Chapter	Reading Topics	Preparing to Read
INTRODUCTION: MECHANICS Page xii		
1. READING SKILLS AND STRATEGIES Page 9		• Making predictions about the text • Exploring what you already know • Asking questions about the text
2. FIRE! Page 27	1. The Elements of Fire 2. Fighting Fire with Fire 3. The Great Chicago Fire 4. Keeping an Eye on Coal Fires	• Making predictions about the text • Exploring what you already know • Asking questions about the text
3. THE EXTRAORDINARY SHARK Page 42	1. Some Basic Facts About Sharks 2. Shark Sense 3. Fish Stories 4. Shark Sinks Teeth into Teen	• Making predictions about the text • Exploring what you already know • Asking questions about the text
4. ALL ABOUT HAIR Page 57	1. The Importance of Hair 2. Questions and Answers about Hair 3. Hair-Care Products from Your Kitchen 4. Madam C. J. Walker: 19th Century Empress of Hair	• Making predictions about the text • Exploring what you already know • Asking questions about the text
5. READING SKILLS AND STRATEGIES Page 73		• Making predictions about the text

6. FOOD ON THE RUN Page 92	1. The Growth of Fast Food in the United States
	2. Nutritional Charts
	3. Man Sues Fast-Food Companies for Health Problems
	4. Letters to the Editor:
	  (1) Americans are taking over the world with hamburgers!
	  (2) Don't Blame the Americans
		• Making predictions about the text

Reading	Remembering	Vocabulary Strategies
• Skimming for gist • Scanning		
• Marking the text • Reading more than once • Using connectors (*I, you, he, she, it, we, they*) to follow ideas • Using signal words to predict ideas	• Using pictures	• Deciding which words are important • Looking for internal definitions • Using synonyms, antonyms, and restatements
• Marking the text • Reading more than once • Using connectors (*I, you, he, she, it, we, they*) to follow ideas • Using signal words to predict ideas	• Using pictures	• Deciding which words are important • Looking for internal definitions • Using synonyms, antonyms, and restatements
• Marking the text • Reading more than once • Using connectors (*I, you, he, she, it, we, they*) to follow ideas • Using signal words to predict ideas	• Using pictures	• Deciding which words are important • Looking for internal definitions • Using synonyms, antonyms, and restatements
• Marking the text • Reading more than once • Using connectors (*I, you, he, she, it, we, they*) to follow ideas • Using signal words to predict ideas	• Using pictures	• Deciding which words are important • Looking for internal definitions • Using synonyms, antonyms, and restatements
• Identifying the main idea • Using connectors (*this, that, these, those, there, one*) to follow ideas • Using signal words to predict ideas	• Using graphic organizers	• Using grammar • Using word forms • Using world knowledge
• Identifying the main idea • Using connectors (*this, that, these, those, there, one*) to follow ideas • Using signal words to predict ideas	• Using graphic organizers	• Using grammar • Using word forms • Using world knowledge

Chapter	Reading Topics	Preparing to Read
7. UNDERGROUND WORLD Page 110	1. Modern Geology: Some Cave Basics 2. Caving Equipment 3. To Save a Cave 4. One Man's Dream	• Making predictions about the text
8. NUMBERS, NUMBERS, NUMBERS Page 128	1. Making Sense of Numbers 2. The Abacus 3. The Importance of Nothing 4. Mayan Numerals	• Making predictions about the text
9. READING SKILLS AND STRATEGIES Page 144		• Predicting from first and last paragraphs
10. ALONG THE SILK ROAD Page 164	1. The Silk Road: Romantic but Misnamed 2. The Adventures of Marco Polo—Fact or Fiction? 3. SILK 4. Take a Silk Road Adventure!	• Predicting from first and last paragraphs
11. HURRAY FOR HOLLYWOOD! Page 185	1. The Sign of the Stars: A History of a Famous Landmark 2. Glossary of Movie Credits 3. Careerline 4. Meet Me at the Red Pagoda	• Predicting from first and last paragraphs
12. BRIDGES Page 202	1. London Bridge Is a Tourist Attraction in Arizona 2. Types of Bridges 3. The Akashi Kaikyo Bridge: The Longest Suspension Bridge in the World 4. The Collapse of Galloping Gertie	• Predicting from first and last paragraphs

Appendix 1   Scanning Practice   220
Appendix 2   Skimming Practice   225

Reading	Remembering	Vocabulary Strategies
• Identifying the main idea • Using connectors (*this, that, these, those, there, one*) to follow ideas • Using signal words to predict ideas	• Using graphic organizers	• Using grammar • Using word forms • Using world knowledge
• Identifying the main idea • Using connectors (*this, that, these, those, there, one*) to follow ideas • Using signal words to predict ideas	• Using graphic organizers	• Using grammar • Using word forms • Using world knowledge
• Understanding supporting details • Using connectors (ellipses) to follow ideas • Using signal words to predict ideas • Making inferences • Reading difficult material	• Outlining	• Using grouping and classification • Using a dictionary • Understanding abbreviations
• Understanding supporting details • Using connectors (ellipses) to follow ideas • Using signal words to predict ideas • Making inferences • Reading difficult material	• Outlining	• Using grouping and classification • Using a dictionary • Understanding abbreviations
• Understanding supporting details • Using connectors (ellipses) to follow ideas • Using signal words to predict ideas • Making inferences • Reading difficult material	• Outlining	• Using grouping and classification • Using a dictionary • Understanding abbreviations
• Understanding supporting details • Using connectors (ellipses) to follow ideas • Using signal words to predict ideas • Making inferences • Reading difficult material	• Outlining	• Using grouping and classification • Using a dictionary • Understanding abbreviations

Acknowledgements

I would like to thank the instructors who reviewed **ReadSmart** during the development of the series for their insightful comments and suggestions.

I would also like to thank Thomas Healy for supporting **ReadSmart** from its inception, Susan Johnson for her invaluable improvements to my ideas, and Annie Sullivan for taking a working manuscript and turning it into a book.

Cheryl Pavlik

To the Teacher

ReadSmart is a three-level reading skills series featuring an innovative approach to reading development. Extensive reading and vocabulary skills instruction chapters, followed by ample opportunities to practice the target skills, help learners to **read smart**.

Features

- **Skills and strategies chapters** present and practice vital **reading strategies,** such as using signal words to predict ideas, and **reading skills,** such as skimming and scanning.
- **Vocabulary strategies,** such as recognizing internal definitions, using synonyms, antonyms, and restatements, and using word forms, help learners to read more fluently.
- **Reading chapters** provide numerous diverse opportunities for learners to practice and apply the target skills and strategies.
- **Self-evaluation activities** make learners aware of the skills and strategies they use when reading.
- **A wide range of reading genres,** including textbook excerpts, magazine features, newspaper articles, encyclopedia entries, and dictionary entries, prepares students for academic reading as well as reading for pleasure.
- **A skills chart** is included in the table of contents of each book.
- **Chapter quizzes** in the Teacher's Manual prepare students for different types of test-taking situations, including standardized multiple choice, matching, true/false, and questions where students must apply the reading strategies and skills to a text.
- **A Teacher's Manual** provides an overview for the teacher, chapter quizzes, and complete answer keys.
- **An optional audio program** with recorded reading passages provides expansion opportunities for teachers.

Components

- **Student Book** has 12 units: three skills and strategies chapters that present and practice both reading and vocabulary skills and strategies, and nine reading chapters that provide diverse opportunities for learners to practice and apply the target skills and strategies.

- **Teacher's Manual** provides the following:
  - Teaching tips and techniques
  - Answer keys for the Student Book
  - Expansion activities
  - Chapter quizzes in a variety of test formats, such as standardized multiple choice, matching, true/false, and questions where students must apply the reading strategies and skills to a text
  - Answer keys for the chapter quizzes.
- **Audio program** contains recordings of the readings in both audio CD and audiocassette formats.

About the Series

ReadSmart is a three-level reading skills series intended for high beginning, intermediate, and high intermediate students who are studying English. The topics, reading genres, and strategies were purposefully chosen to accommodate the needs and interests of a wide variety of students. Although most of the readings are non-academic in nature, each topic is related to an academic discipline. Therefore, the series can be used with students who would like to read more effectively for academic, career, or general purposes.

The Philosophy

ReadSmart teaches that there is no single correct way to read. Some strategies work well for some people and not others. Some strategies work well in some situations and not others. The key to success is using the right strategy in each reading situation. Effective readers understand this, and they use a number of different reading strategies with great flexibility. Effective readers are not easily discouraged. If one strategy doesn't work, they simply try another. *ReadSmart* therefore introduces students to a great variety of reading and vocabulary strategies. The text then encourages readers to be flexible by providing them with opportunities to practice different strategies in the readings.

The readings represent different topics, genres, and styles. They were carefully chosen to provide reading practice at different levels of difficulty. Some readings may seem relatively easy. These will help students gain confidence and give them a chance to practice the reading skills and strategies in depth. Other readings will be quite challenging, allowing students to see how much they can understand when faced with difficult material. Although the chapters were designed to move generally from easier to more difficult, each reading chapter also offers a mixture of levels of difficulty. For this reason, a reading in Chapter 7 might be easier than a reading in Chapter 4, for example. However, within each chapter, the most challenging reading is last. This structure allows students to gain a fair amount of background knowledge before they tackle more difficult material.

The Reading Process

One of the most important lessons that students studying English have to learn is that reading is not a linear process. Effective readers usually do not begin at the first word in a text and continue without stopping until the end—especially if the reading is challenging. The reading process is much more flexible than that. Effective readers often begin **the reading process** before they actually begin reading and, in some cases, they may start at the end. Then as they are reading, they constantly move forward and backward—predicting, making deductions, checking their guesses, and reacting to the information they are learning.

The reading process does not always go smoothly, and there are often words or sentences that the reader may not completely understand. Effective readers are willing to keep reading, even though they may be confused. They continue to read while looking for clues to help them understand the text.

ReadSmart encourages students to "read through" their confusion and then reread to increase their understanding. Students learn that understanding *approximately* what a word means is often enough. For example, depending on your purpose for reading, it may be enough to know that a carburetor is a part of car engine without having any idea what it does. Read the following sentence:

> The garage was filled with things that Adam had collected over the years and discarded: an old lawn mower, broken sports equipment, unused tools, cans of dried-up paint, even an old carburetor.

In this sentence, you only need to know that a carburetor is a concrete noun that one might find in a garage.

Reflective Reading and Self Evaluation

Research has shown that **reflective reading** is one of the keys to reading improvement. For this reason, every reading chapter in *ReadSmart* concludes with a section that asks students to review their own reading process, identify the strategies that they used, evaluate their effectiveness, and think about what they might do differently in the future. Students have many opportunities to compare their work with a partner's. The purpose of these activities is to help students share their reading experiences and exchange ideas about the use of the different strategies.

Text Overview

Introduction

Each text begins with an introductory chapter on the mechanics of reading. This chapter provides practice in the physical skills required for scanning and skimming. The exercises focus on things such as rapid eye movement, using your hand to move down the page, and so on.

Skills and Strategies Chapters (1, 5, 9)

There are three **Skills and Strategies chapters** in the text (Chapters 1, 5, and 9). These chapters present skills and strategies for improving your reading. Skills and strategies for comprehension are taught in Part 1; skills and strategies for understanding vocabulary are taught in Part 2. The comprehension section is further divided into steps in the reading process: *Prepare, Read,* and *Remember.* Although **ReadSmart** teaches that reading is not necessarily a linear process, these chapters do teach and practice skills and strategies in a logical progression to ensure that students have mastered them in isolation before applying them.

Each strategy is introduced, explained, and then practiced. The exercises in these chapters are controlled so that students benefit from focused practice of individual skills and strategies. Especially useful strategies, such as using signal words to predict ideas, are taught and recycled in every skills/strategies chapter with different material.

Thematic Reading Chapters (2, 3, 4, 6, 7, 8, 10, 11, 12)

There are nine **Reading chapters** in the text (Chapters 2-4, 6-8, and 10-12). Each reading chapter contains four readings on a single topic. The activities accompanying the readings are designed specifically to target the comprehension and vocabulary skills and strategies that students learned in the previous skills/strategies chapter. But rather than provide additional focused practice of individual strategies, the reading chapters ask students to apply the skills and strategies in powerful combinations as they read. As the text progresses, skills and strategies are recycled in the reading chapters naturally.

The reading chapters open with a topical photo and discussion questions. These tools activate students' background knowledge about the topic and prompt them into thinking about the topic in a general way. The four readings in the chapter expand the steps in the reading process: *Prepare, Read, Read Again, Remember,* and *Discuss.*

The comprehension and vocabulary skills and strategies taught in the skills/strategies chapters are embedded in the reading steps. *Post-reading Activities* focus students' attention more closely on strategies appropriate for each reading.

Reviewing Your Reading prompts students to reflect on the strategies that they used in each reading.

Appendices

The appendices provide extra reading practice in scanning and skimming. In Appendix 1, students scan realistic items, such as a television schedule, a bus schedule, a class schedule, and a menu, looking for specific information. In Appendix 2, students skim short readings to grasp main ideas and key points.

Introduction

The Mechanics of Reading: Scanning and Skimming

You may be surprised to learn this fact about reading: There are different ways to do it. You may read every word, but you can also read groups of words, certain types of words, or particular sentences. The best method depends on the text and your purpose. Scanning and skimming are two common methods of finding information quickly.

Scanning

Scanning is reading quickly to find specific information. This is a reading skill that you use every day. You scan texts to find a phone number, locate a name, or look up a word in a dictionary.

Understanding the Strategy

Scanning is especially useful for certain types of text and reading situations. The basic method for every type of text is the same.

Search for the shape of words or phrases as well as their meaning.

Scanning Method

You search for the answer to a specific question. Your eyes search for **recognition**. They look for shapes of certain letters, numbers, or whole words. Your mind searches for **meanings**. It looks for the connections of the letters, numbers, or whole words—exact words or synonyms—to the question. You make your eyes move very quickly.

Examples

A. Text: School admissions essay for Sally Jones
Question: Where did Sally go to high school?

Search for:

- shapes and size of capital letters (that begin proper nouns): B, U, H
- question-related words: went to, graduated, finished, school, high school, study
- specific names of places: El Paso High School, New Martinsville High School

B. Text: Store advertisement
Question: When does the store open every day?

Search for:

- shapes of numbers and letters with time punctuation: 10:00, 8:30, 12:30 A.M., P.M.
- question-related words: morning, evenings, days of week, noon, hours, close
- specific times or dates: Opens 9:00 A.M., Monday–Friday

Commonly Scanned Texts

Most people scan the same types of material. Examine the following list.

- a page of movie ads in a newspaper
- a weather map
- a list of sports scores
- a bus or train schedule
- a menu
- the label on a can or box of food
- a table of contents for a magazine or book

ACTIVITY 1   Scan for the word in bold. Move your eyes quickly across the line. Circle the word each time you see it.

1. **possible**	passable	possible	passable	plausible	possible	probable	passable
2. **made**	made	make	maid	made	make	mood	made
3. **think**	thank	think	tank	think	thank	thin	tank
4. **night**	night	might	might	night	neat	might	night
5. **touch**	cough	tough	touch	touch	torch	cough	touch
6. **tried**	tired	tried	tired	tries	tires	tried	tired
7. **calm**	calm	clam	clamp	calm	clam	calm	clam
8. **biology**	biologist	biology	biologist	biological	biology	botany	biologist
9. **peach**	peace	peach	preach	peach	peace	piece	preach
10. **reading**	reading	railing	rapping	riding	reading	riding	rapping

ACTIVITY 2

Scan for the term in bold. Move your eyes quickly across the line. Circle the term each time you see it. Some may not have a match.

1. **telephone**	telegraph	Teleprompter	Telephone	telegraph	Television	telephone
2. **10:32 A.M.**	10:32 P.M.	10.32	1032	10:32 A.M.	1032!	10:23 A.M.
3. **CO**	CD	OH	CO	OC	OD	DO
4. **1,932**	19.32	1932	193.20	11,932	1,932	119.32
5. **32° C**	23° C	32° F	32° C	32°	32° F	32° C
6. **information**	informative	informer	instruction	informácion	infiltrate	inform
7. **GSU**	LSU	SUL	GSU	GUS	G$U	OSU
8. **electrical**	electoral	elected	electricity	electrical	elected	electoral
9. **March 1**	Marsh 3	March 1	May 11	Marke 1	1 March	March 11
10. **4,057.89**	4,054.89	4,507.89	4,057.49	4,987.89	4,057,88.	4,057.89

ACTIVITY 3

Scan the lists for the phrase in bold. Circle each phrase when you find it. Remember: Work quickly!

1. **practice reading faster**

practice riding more
private reading rooms
Patsy reads faster
physical relief works
practice reading faster
playtime stays forever
painters working over
princess rising fair
practice piano more
practice reading faster
private reading rooms
physical relief works
painters working over
practice reading faster

practice reading faster
playtime stays forever
princess rising fair
practice reading faster
Patsy reads faster
practice riding more
pandas roam better
practice reading faster
painters working over
princess rising fair
Patsy reads faster
pandas roam better
practice reading faster
physical relief works

2. the small red brick house

the small red-haired mouse	the small red wood house
these small brick houses	the simple red brick house
the small boy's red horse	the small red brick house
the Smalls' red brick house	the smart red-haired horse
the small red brick house	those smart red British hotels
the small red wood house	the small boy's red horse
the simple red bridge house	these small brick houses
the smart red-haired horse	the small red-haired mouse
the small red brick house	the Smalls' red brick house
those smart red British hotels	the small red brick house
the simple red bick house	these small brick houses

ACTIVITY 4   Scan each text to find the information asked for.

1. Scan this weather map. Find:

   a. the temperature in Cleveland. _____   c. the coldest city on this day. _____

   b. the weather in Miami. _____   d. the hottest city on this day. _____

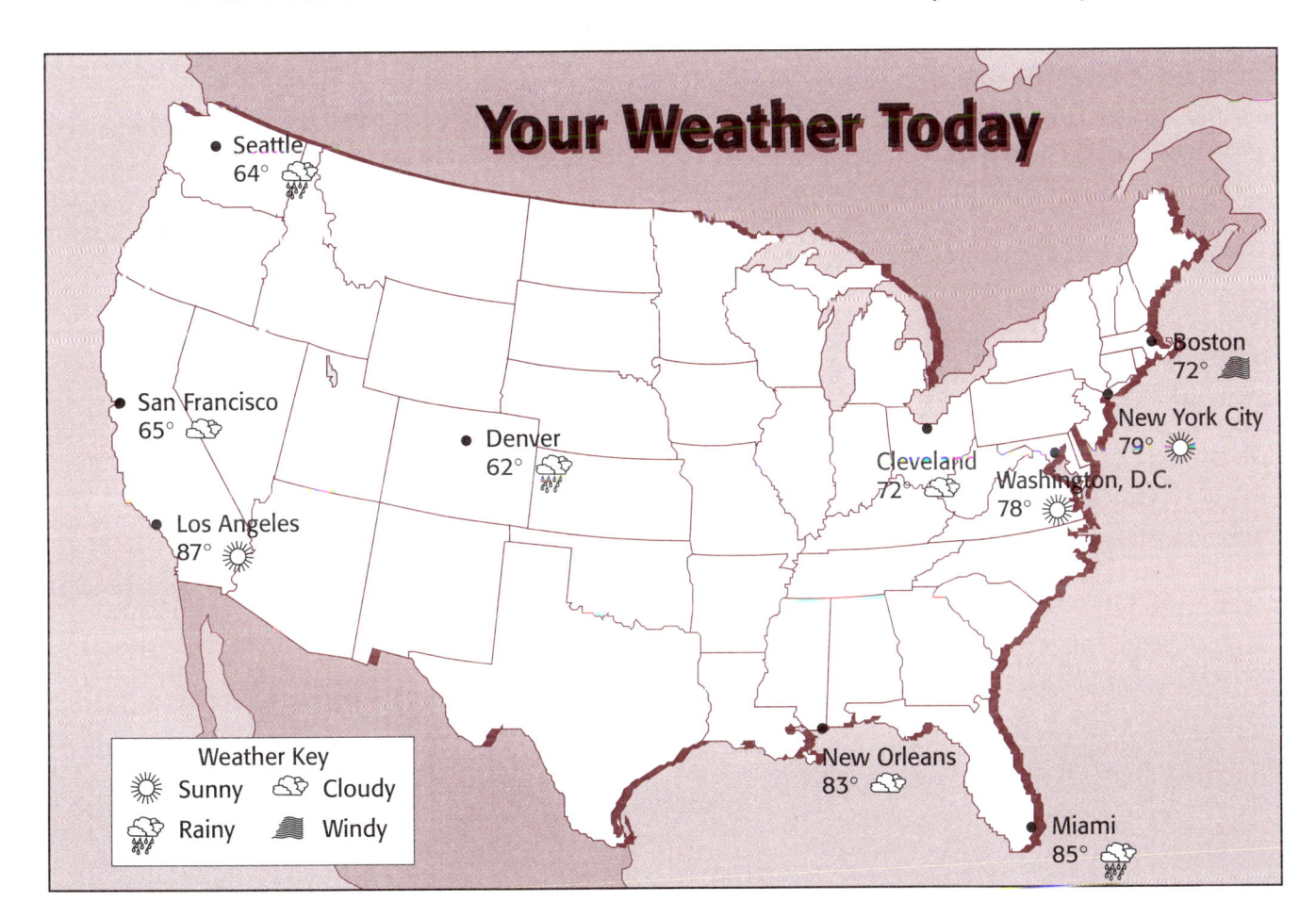

Your Weather Today

- Seattle 64° (Rainy)
- San Francisco 65° (Cloudy)
- Los Angeles 87° (Sunny)
- Denver 62° (Rainy)
- Cleveland 72° (Cloudy)
- Boston 72° (Windy)
- New York City 79° (Sunny)
- Washington, D.C. 78° (Sunny)
- New Orleans 83° (Cloudy)
- Miami 85° (Rainy)

Weather Key
- Sunny
- Cloudy
- Rainy
- Windy

2. Scan this table of contents from a magazine. Find the articles on the following subjects.

	Title	Page
a. how to be a sports announcer		
b. what makes a great coach		
c. Sam Cooper		

Sports World

December 2000   Volume 22 Issue 14

TABLE OF CONTENTS

LETTERS TO THE EDITOR 20

A BASKETBALL LEGEND 33
Sam Cooper is probably the best basketball player in the history of the sport. Find out how a legend is made.

THE ART OF SPORTS ANNOUNCING 56
Would you like to be a sports announcer? Jack Davis, longtime baseball announcer, talks about his job and tells us how to get started.

WORLD CUP UPDATE 78
Samantha McGregor reports on the latest matches and makes some predictions for the next World Cup.

NEW SPORTS 92
This month Carol Kimball reports on parasailing.

WHAT MAKES A GREAT COACH 108
Adam Asher interviews athletes, psychologists, and coaches to try to discover the characteristics of a great coach.

KIDS AND ORGANIZED SPORTS 115
You often hear about parents behaving badly at their children's sporting events. How often does this happen and how does it affect young children?

3. Scan this section of the telephone yellow pages. Find the following information.

   a. what kind of business Frazier & Son is _____

   b. the phone number of Green Mountain Interiors _____

   c. when Furniture Plus is open _____

   d. who sells Englander mattresses _____

4. Scan the following paragraph. Find the following information.

   a. what an avalanche contains   _____

   b. where the avalanche happened   _____

   c. how fast an avalanche can move   _____

> In April 1981, a million tons of snow crashed eight miles down Mount Sanford in Alaska, creating a cloud of snow dust that could be seen 100 miles away. It was one of history's largest avalanches. Amazingly, no one was hurt. Luckily, avalanches that big are rare. A moving mass of snow, an avalanche may contain ice, soil, rocks, and even trees. An avalanche begins when an unstable mass of snow breaks away from a mountainside. The mass begins to slide downhill, and moves more quickly as it slides. Some avalanches can move as quickly as 245 miles an hour—about four times as fast as the speediest downhill skier.

Skimming

Skimming is reading quickly to grasp main ideas. There are many reasons to skim a text.

- saving time: to get the basics if you are in a hurry
- reviewing: to remember key points in material you have already read
- researching: to find out if a text will be useful to your report

When you skim, you comprehend approximately 50 percent of a text. You grasp the main ideas, not the details. In which situations should you *not* skim the text?

- reading a recipe for a dish you are cooking
- reading instructions on how to use your new computer
- studying material for a history essay exam
- learning a poem

Understanding the Strategy

Main ideas are often stated in introductions and conclusions. Various ways are used to skim a text. Following are two basic ways to do it.

Ignore unfamiliar words. Search only for key ideas.

Whole Text Method

- Read the title, headings, and sub-headings.
- Note pictures, charts, or graphs.
- Read the topic sentence, or the first and last sentence, of each paragraph.
- For short texts, quickly move your eyes over every line.

Beginning and Ending Method

- Read the title, headings, and sub-headings.
- Note pictures, charts, or graphs.
- Read the introduction: the first few lines or the first paragraph.
- Read the conclusion: the last few lines or the last paragraph.

ACTIVITY 5   Skim the restaurant review. Choose the best title.

a. Hamburger Heaven: The Place for Healthy Family Fun
b. Looking for Fun? Go to Hamburger Heaven
c. Need Peace and Quiet? Try Hamburger Heaven

Hamburger Heaven opened just three weeks ago. Its owner, Greta Bouchet, is also the owner of the very popular Greta's Garden. The two restaurants couldn't be more different. Greta's Garden serves healthy, vegetarian meals in a small but beautiful setting filled with flowers and live birds. The mood is calm and quiet. Hamburger Heaven is the exact opposite. The menu is amazing, but not very healthy and certainly not vegetarian. There are 25 different kinds of hamburgers and 6 kinds of French fries, along with onion rings and other high-fat foods. And the surroundings are anything but calm and quiet. The walls are purple and pink, and the music is loud. The surroundings really wake you up! One thing, however, that these two restaurants have in common—they both serve delicious food. So, if you're feeling healthy and are looking for peace and quiet, try Greta's Garden. But when you're really hungry and want a rousing good time, go to Hamburger Heaven.

ACTIVITY 6   Skim the brief newspaper article. Choose the best title.

a. Scientists Find Pets in Mummies' Tombs
b. Animals Found Buried with Egyptian Mummies
c. Sacred Egyptian Animals

International

Recently, scientists have discovered that Egyptians also mummified animals. Some of the animals found in tombs were pets such as cats, dogs, and rabbits. Scientists believe that the animals were mummified by the same technique used for humans. Apparently, the early Egyptians had many household pets and were quite fond of them. They believed their pets would continue into the afterlife to protect and comfort their masters.

However, other animals have also been discovered. In other tombs, the mummies' bulls and crocodiles were found. For the ancient Egyptians, these animals were sacred and were the living spirits of gods. The Egyptians took good care of them while they were alive, and when they died, they buried them like kings.

ACTIVITY 7

Skim the article. Choose the best title.

a. Why is a Résumé Important?
b. Writing a Résumé: Remember This!
c. Write a Great Résumé in Fifteen Minutes!

Writing a résumé is serious business. It is usually the first picture of you that an employer sees. If the résumé isn't good, it will be the only one that he sees. A good résumé can get you an interview and possibly the job of your dreams.

The questions is: What is a good résumé? Many of us have difficulty writing about ourselves. What do we say? What shouldn't we say? Whatever you say, remember this key point: A good résumé shows how you can help the employer. Think about advertisements. They ask you to buy a product. Do they tell you that the company needs your money? Of course not. A good ad shows you that *you need the product*. Your résumé needs to show the employer that he needs you.

ACTIVITY 8

Skim the article. Choose the best title.

a. Bicycles are Unsafe
b. The Benefits of Bicycling
c. Making Money on Your Bicycle

Most Americans realize that biking is excellent exercise, offering several health benefits. However, most of us only ride our bikes for fun or sport. If you don't ride for more practical purposes, you are missing some of the best benefits of biking. For example, biking to work helps you save money on gas. A tank of gas for your car can cost $50.00 a week, and more if you drive a long way to work.

Biking also helps you help keep the environment clean. Your car chokes the air with terrible chemicals, but your bike will not. Use your bike more often and help others as well as yourself. Do simple errands such as going to a nearby post office or convenience store on your bicycle. Leave your car at home when you can. You'll save money on gas and help the environment, too.

Reading Skills and Strategies

Overview of the Strategies

PART 1

Comprehension Strategies

Prepare
- Making Predictions about the Text
- Exploring What You Already Know
- Asking Questions about the Text

Read
- Marking the Text
- Reading More than Once
- Using Connectors (Personal Pronouns) to Follow Ideas
- Using Signal Words to Predict Ideas

Remember
- Using Pictures

PART 2

Vocabulary Strategies
- Deciding Which Words Are Important
- Looking for Internal Definitions
- Using Synonyms, Antonyms, and Restatements

PART 1. COMPREHENSION STRATEGIES

Prepare

Making Predictions about the Text

Effective readers prepare to read. They try to predict what's in a text before they read it. Why? Predicting helps prepare you for the information in the text. Good readers are good predictors.

The first thing to predict is the **topic** of the text.

Predict the topic before you begin to read.

Understanding the Strategy

Before reading the text, look at its **features**. The features reveal information about content. Each of the following items is a feature of a text. Topics can best be predicted from titles and/or visuals and charts.

Features

- title(s)
- pictures and charts
- length of the article
- name and title or position of the author
- style (general order or appearance of information)
- vocabulary and language

Example

Where Does the Money Go?
A Three-Part Series on Taxes and Spending

by Janice Freeman

SPRINGFIELD—Everyone complains about high taxes. However, few people know how the government spends their tax money.

How We Spend Your Taxes

Service	Percentage
Education	50%
Roads and Highways	15%
Hospitals	10%
Social Services	20%
Libraries	5%

Percentage of Your Tax Dollars

TOPIC: How the government spends your tax money

The title says the article is about money. However, what does the article *say* about money? The subtitle and the graph give more information. Together, the title, subtitle, and graph reveal the specific topic: how the government spends tax money.

ACTIVITY 1   Look at the titles and/or pictures for each text. Predict the topic.

Kicking the Cigarette Habit

By TOBY WILLIAMS
Banner Staff

JACKSON—The Healthnow Quit Line and the Utah Department of Health are encouraging couples to quit smoking this Valentine's Day. "Stop together and keep your romance burning," says Dr. Margie Jasper, director of the Quit Line.

TOPIC: _____

Earth Sciences

Chapter 2: Layers of the Earth

SOIL
Types of Soil

Vegetation and plant life depend on soil. The type of soil you find in a given geography is closely related to climate and vegetation zones. Rock breaks up in chemical and physical reactions to create different types of soil (see right).

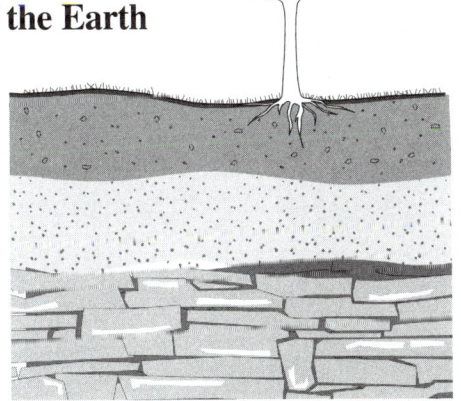

TOPIC: _____

Exploring What You Already Know

Recall what you know about the topic. Your knowledge may be general. It may even be incorrect. However, you may know more than you think.

Another thing to predict is the **language** of the text.

Understanding the Strategy

Exploring helps you recall information about the topic. You can then predict specific words and ideas that might be in a text. This way, it is easier to figure out new words.
Following is a method for exploring what you know.

Explore your knowledge of the topic.

1. Predict the topic. Be very specific.
2. Brainstorm. Think of connected situations and your own experience.
3. Make notes. Note memories, facts, or what you imagine might be true.
4. Write down as much in English as you can.

Example

Pretend you are going to read this article: "How to Purchase a CD Player: Buying a Great Player in Five Easy Steps." Work with a partner to do the following steps.

1. Predict the topic. First, study the title. Guess the meaning of *purchase* from the subtitle. If you can't guess, check a dictionary.

   Be specific. The topic is not "CDs" and it is not "buying a CD." Specifically, it is "five steps to buying a great CD player." What will the five steps be?

2. Explore the topic. Take a moment to brainstorm. Think about *purchasing* or *buying*, and about *CDs*. What do you do before buying a CD player or other things? As you buy? What did you, a friend, or your family do? What would five steps be?

3. Make notes. Jot down the facts or memories that you recalled. Don't write full sentences. Use words in your own language if you need to.

   Example note (fact): <u>Music must sound good. Step 1 = test player!</u>

   Now think of at least three more ideas. Write your ideas in the space below.

   _____

   _____

   _____

4. Translate your notes into English, as much as possible. Also, try to remember English lessons or conversations connected to the topic. Write down any English term you recall.

   Examples: price, play, cost, listen, stereo, sound, song, volume

   Think of at least three more words. Write them on the line below.

   _____

ACTIVITY 2   Work with a partner. Predict words and ideas in the article: "U.S. Announces Plans for Mission to Mars." Follow the four steps listed above. Compare your list with a partner's.

Asking Questions about the Text

"What am I going to learn?" Asking questions about the information in a text is another way to predict. It has a special effect. It helps you prepare to "listen" to the text when you read it.

A third thing to predict is the **content** of the text.

Understanding the Strategy

Ask questions about content, and read to find answers. Try to "listen" to what the text is saying. Following is a method for predicting what you will learn.

Think of questions to ask about the content of the text.

1. Ask yourself: What is the text going to say about the topic?
2. Look at the features of the text. Skim the text. You may skim a little or a lot.
3. Consider specific information the article could give on the topic.
4. Think of wh- questions to ask the author.
5. Write your questions in your notebook.

Wh- questions are questions that use question words beginning with a "w" or an "h". Not all question words apply to every reading. Study this list, and then think of your own:

Who	Where	How many
What	Why	How often
When	How	What kind

CHAPTER 1

ACTIVITY 3 — Read the titles and the first few sentences of each reading. Then do the following steps for each reading.

1. Write three questions the reading may answer. Exchange with a partner.
2. Decide if your partner's questions will be answered. Explain why or why not.
3. Together, develop one more question the reading could answer.

A.

Tree by tree, person by person, Wangari Maathai is making Kenya a better place to live

Wangari Maathai knows the importance of planting seeds. She has ever since she was a little girl. She was born and raised in Nyeri, a farming community in Kenya. Since then, her interest in the environment has gone in many directions.

1. _____
2. _____
3. _____

B.

A New Eye in the Sky

NASA is looking to put a new eye in the sky. They are sending a brand-new telescope into space. The James Webb Telescope will see farther than all other telescopes. When the Webb goes into space in 2010, it will see even farther than the Hubble Telescope.

1. _____
2. _____
3. _____

C.

> **First Ladies to Fight Poverty**
>
> **Twenty-two First Ladies from North, South, and Central America Promise to Fight Child Poverty**
>
> U.S. First Lady Laura Bush joined 21 other wives of world leaders at a conference held September 26, 2002, in Mexico. There, the First Ladies promised to fight child poverty in their nations. Mrs. Bush said the fight must take place not only in poor, developing countries but also in the United States.

1. _____
2. _____
3. _____

Read

Marking the Text

After predicting, you begin reading. When you read, read actively. Effective readers do more than move their eyes across a page. They communicate with the text. Many college textbooks have wide margins for this reason. The extra space gives students room to "talk" to the text.

Understanding the Strategy

Marking a text helps you understand, or process, what you read. Use some of the common marks listed below, and develop your own special marks.

Talk to the text: Read with a pencil in hand.

Common ways to mark a text:

- Use question marks in the margin for difficult sections.
- Circle important new words.
- Use an exclamation point (!) for opinions you agree with.
- Write a note in the margin where you do not agree.
- Number items in a list such as steps in a process or reasons.

ACTIVITY 4   Read the text one time. As you read, mark the text using the strategies listed on page 15.

A Teacher's Job

1   There are several reasons to learn a language, but most adults are studying by choice. This makes most adult students enthusiastic and motivated learners—a very nice experience for a teacher. However, these students can also be a challenge to teachers. Since they're studying by choice, if they are not enjoying themselves, they may just walk away.

5   It is the teacher's job to keep these students interested. To be successful, a teacher must be knowledgeable, sensitive, and creative. Creativity is particularly important. Teachers must find ways for students to practice real English in the classroom. There are many benefits of classroom practice. First, of course, students have the opportunity to practice the language they are learning. In addition, many people learn better in a social environment. They are also more likely to continue with the class if they feel part of a group.

Reading More than Once

Always read a foreign-language text more than once. In fact, you should read any text that you are trying to learn more than once. Each time you read, you learn more.

Understanding the Strategy

Each reading gives you more, and different, information about the text. Generally, the first reading is for main ideas. Each succeeding reading is for the details.

Read more than once, and read differently every time.

The first time you read:

- get whatever you can. Don't worry about the points you don't understand.
- look for answers to the questions you have in mind.
- notice unfamiliar vocabulary words, but don't look them up or even try to figure them out.

The second time you read:

- underline important ideas.
- read more slowly and carefully.
- look for answers to more questions.
- mark difficult sections.

The third time you read:

- read for specific details.
- pay particular attention to difficult sections.
- decide if you need to use a dictionary for words you can't figure out.

The fourth time you read:

- take notes from the text.

ACTIVITY 5   Read the text in Activity 4 a second, third, and fourth time. Use the strategies listed on page 16. Compare texts with a partner. Discuss these questions and then write the answers.

1. What is the topic? What did you know about it? _____

_____

2. Which parts were easy to understand? Why? _____

_____

3. What parts were difficult to understand? Why? _____

_____

4. Name some English words you expected to see in this reading. _____

_____

5. Did the fourth reading help you? Why or why not? _____

_____

Using Connectors to Follow Ideas

It is easy to get lost in a text. However, you won't get lost if you learn to use connectors to follow ideas. The sentences in a passage should connect to other sentences before **or** after them. Sometimes they connect to sentences both before **and** after them.

Understanding the Strategy

Pronouns are a common way to connect sentences. To follow ideas through personal pronouns, first think about basic facts.

Follow ideas through personal pronouns.

Type:	personal
	singular: *I, you, he, she, it*
	plural: *we, you, they*
Location:	before or after referent
Referent (or antecedent):	The referent can be a person, animal, place, or thing (object, idea, situation) that the pronoun represents.

It can be "empty," that is, not refer to a specific noun. We often use an "empty *it*" to talk about time and weather.

    It's three o'clock.   It's rainy in April.

However, other types of statements are also common.

    It's not easy to learn to ski.

18 CHAPTER 1

ACTIVITY 6 Work as a class. Name the referent of each underlined personal pronoun. One has no referent. Explain why.

Dave and I walked out to the field. We̲ saw a young black horse running beside a strong
                                      1

white mare. He̲ was beautiful, and so was she̲. They̲ ran through the field and crossed it̲
            2   3   4   5

very quickly! It̲ was a warm and sunny day, one we̲ will always remember.
              6   7

1. We _____

2. He _____

3. she _____

4. They _____

5. it _____

6. It _____

7. we _____

ACTIVITY 7 Draw arrows from the underlined personal pronouns to their referents. Put an "X" over any without a referent.

1. Sam named his car "Rosie." He̲ says she̲ is the best car in town.

2. My dog is unusual. He̲ can sing and play cards.

3. Many people in my school don't take the bus. They̲ prefer to walk or drive.

4. It̲ can be difficult to move to a new town.

5. Jack and I were friends, but after he̲ moved away, we̲ didn't see each other again.

6. What time is it̲?

7. Marge and Mike went to Carol's party, but they̲ didn't take her̲ a present. She won't invite them again.

8. Farmers work hard when it̲ isn't raining. However, they̲ hate bad weather because it often ruins their crops.

Using Signal Words to Predict Ideas

Like pronouns, signal words connect sentences. They also connect information within a sentence. Signal words help you predict information that is coming.

Understanding the Strategy

A signal word does not identify exact information. It signals that a certain **type** of idea is coming. For example, *and* adds similar ideas, and *but* shows contrast.

Look for signal words that predict ideas.

Some Types and Examples of Signal Words

Addition: *and, also*
Conclusion: *finally*
Cause or Reason: *because, since*
Contrast: *but, however*
Effect or Result: *consequently*
Example: *for example*

Sample Sentences

Sam went to the store **and** bought a radio.
He **also** bought a television.
The radio was expensive, **but** it didn't work well.
For example, the volume control was broken.
He couldn't return it **because** it was on sale.
Finally, he decided to fix it himself.
However, he discovered that he wasn't a good electrician **since** after he took it apart, he couldn't get it back together.
Consequently, he had to pay a repairman to fix it.

ACTIVITY 8 — Predict the type of information coming next. Complete each passage, and explain your answers to the class.

1. "I'd like to help you *but* _____.

   Is this person going to help you? _____

2. "Jenny isn't going to the party *since* _____.

   What kind of information will come next? _____

3. "Mr. Brathwell gave us the test. Then he graded them. We waited patiently while he wrote the grades in his book. *Finally,* he _____.

   What did the teacher do next? _____

ACTIVITY 9

Note the signal word, and complete each sentence. Circle the letter of the correct answer.

Example

We should save our parks and help the environment. However,
- a. many governments are spending a lot of money on the parks.
- (b.) some people say that using the land for business is more important.
- c. the rain forests are beautiful.

1. Scientists often try to explain difficult ideas, but
   - a. people understand more about the world.
   - b. they write articles, and give talks.
   - c. people are too busy to pay attention.

2. Everyone must work to save the earth because
   - a. everyone is doing it.
   - b. nature can save the earth.
   - c. there is so much to do, we must work together.

3. In order to succeed, we must be willing to spend money and
   - a. dollars.
   - b. work hard.
   - c. keep it.

4. We needed to begin years ago but did not. Consequently,
   - a. the job will be quite difficult.
   - b. many people don't like cleaning up the earth.
   - c. we didn't understand the problem well.

5. It's not an impossible task. For example,
   - a. we have already saved many animals.
   - b. no one can help us.
   - c. the rain forests are dying.

ACTIVITY 10

Work with a partner to complete each sentence. Make three predictions for each. Compare yours with another pair's.

Example:

Harry wanted the job. However, _he didn't get it / he didn't apply / he wasn't qualified_.

1. The weather is very cold in the winter and _____.

2. Brazil has won the World Cup many times; however, _____.

3. Don't try to exercise, since _____.

4. Foreign foods are delicious. For example, _____.

5. We spent three hours looking for her. Finally, _____.

6. The writer wrote many stories. He also _____.

Remember

Using Pictures

According to experts, readers often forget what they read. There are several methods that help memory. One of the best is taking picture notes. Picturing helps you see the information in a text.

Understanding the Strategy

Pictures are often used to illustrate descriptions, processes, and instructions or directions. They are simple ways to show ideas. You do not write key information down. Instead, you draw it.

Use pictures to take notes.

Remember

- Do not draw everything, only the most important things.
- If you are in a hurry, abbreviate names and other information.
- Draw simple maps, diagrams, or line drawings.
- Do not try to draw well, only clearly.

Example

Symphony at Foley Tonight

It's easy to get to Foley Auditorium from Cambridge High School. The high school is on the corner of Park and Apple Streets. When you leave the school, turn right onto Park Street. Cross Apple. Walk two more blocks to Kent Avenue. Turn left. Walk one block to Houston Place. The auditorium is at the corner of Kent and Houston.

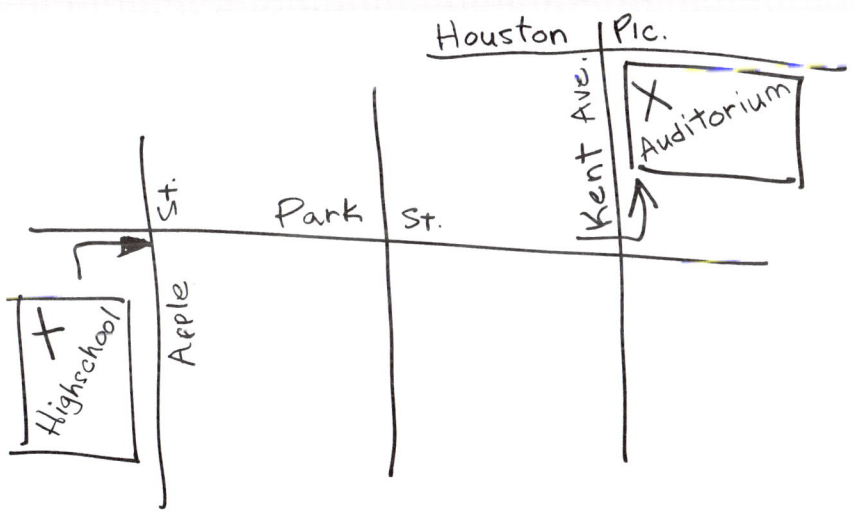

ACTIVITY 11

Read each paragraph and take picture notes. Exchange notes with a partner. Find out if you showed the same information.

1. Each hair on your body grows from a hair *follicle*. A hair follicle is a tiny hole in your skin. The *shaft* is the part of a hair that you see.

2. Each hair shaft has two different layers: the cuticle and the cortex. The *cuticle* is the outside layer. Underneath the cuticle is the *cortex*. The cortex is made of proteins that curl like a telephone cord. Try pulling a hair. When you stretch a hair, you are straightening the proteins in the cortex. When you release the hair, the proteins curl up again.

PART 2 · VOCABULARY STRATEGIES

Deciding Which Words Are Important

Reading in a foreign language can be difficult. There will always be many words you do not know. How should you deal with unfamiliar terms? First, don't try to figure out words that are not important to grasping main ideas.

Understanding the Strategy

To grasp key points, you do not need to understand every word of the text. You only need to understand the important ones.

First decide if an unknown word is important.

Some types of vocabulary may not be key to the main idea.

This can be the case with descriptive words and items in a list.

Examples

Descriptive: Sam ran up the **narrow** stairs. (Sam ran up the stairs.)
Eagles are **savage** killers that have little fear. (Eagles are killers.)

Listed items: I bought apples, **oranges**, and grapes at the grocery store. (I bought fruit.)

In addition to the electric light, Thomas Edison invented the typewriter, the electric generator, and the **mimeograph machine**. (Edison invented many things in addition to the light.)

Capitalized words may not be key to the main idea.

A capital letter doesn't always mean that a word is important. In fact, it is often enough to know that it means a specific person, place, or thing.

Examples

Daniel was the first leader of the Committee to Investigate Environmental Hazards. (Daniel / He was the first leader of the committee.)

Sergeant Leopold Stakowski won the Wendell Wilson Medal of Honor.
(Sergeant Stakowski / He won the medal.)

Repeated words will be key to the main idea.

Topic sentences of paragraphs state main ideas. (See Chapter 5 for identifying topic sentences.) Titles of articles often do, too. The terms in these will be repeated. Expect to see the same words, other forms of the word, or synonyms.

ACTIVITY 12 Read the following paragraph. Only one of the underlined words is key to the main idea. Choose the word, and figure out the meaning.

The Great Plains Buffalo

The buffalo of the Great Plains was a <u>migratory</u> animal. In the autumn, before winter snows covered the <u>frigid</u> northern grasslands, <u>herds</u> of buffalo migrated southward, where there was still green grass in <u>abundance</u>. With the coming of spring, they migrated northward again, <u>grazing</u> as they went. Native American groups such as the <u>Shoshone</u> and the <u>Sioux</u> followed them.

Looking for Internal Definitions

Important words are often defined in the text. **Internal definitions** are usually placed near the new word.

Understanding the Strategy

Following are some of the clues that a definition is coming in the text.

Look for clues that an internal definition is coming.

Repeating and defining

Sometimes the term is repeated and then defined in a succeeding sentence.

> Native Americans collected the seeds of edible plants. An **edible plant** is a plant that you can eat.

Single words or phrases

or	They camped in clearings **or** open places in the forest.
in other words	They camped in clearings, **in other words,** open places in the forest.
that is	They camped in clearings, **that is,** open places in the forest.

Punctuation

a long dash (—)	Native Americans ate pemmican—meat that they pounded into a powder and mixed with berries and fat.
a comma (,) (, . . . ,)	Native Americans lived in lodges, small huts made of earth. Native Americans lived in lodges, small huts made of earth, which protected them from the weather.

ACTIVITY 13

Underline the internal definitions. Circle the words they define.

1. Before each flight, the crew chief, the mechanic who works on the plane, inspects the plane.
2. The pilot then makes his "walk around"—the inspection of the outside of the plane.
3. He received a thousand gold reales, gold coins, for his work.
4. The gauges, or dials, are not correct.
5. The teacher told him that his paper was faultless, in other words, perfect.
6. For the first two years I was a peripatetic teacher. That is, I went to many schools so that I could teach in many types of classrooms.
7. Meteorology, the study of the weather, is very interesting.
8. The company is doing a pilot or test of their new medicine.
9. Your home, your town, the countryside around you is your environment.

Using Synonyms, Antonyms, and Restatements

Synonyms, antonyms, and restatements are another type of internal definition, or alternate definition. They are clues that can help you decide if an unfamiliar term is important.

Understanding the Strategy

Synonyms and Restatements

Synonyms are words that have the same or similar meanings. For example, *big* and *large* are synonyms. They often occur after the key term. Restatements are explanations, phrases, or sentences that state a term in a different way. Clues to these are the same as those for internal definitions.

Find synonyms, antonyms, and restatements that are clues to the meaning of unknown words.

Antonyms

Antonyms are words that have opposite meanings. *Big* and *small* are antonyms. Clues that an antonym is coming can be words that signal a contrast.

Example

It takes days for Mr. Jones to **expound** that theory, but it only takes the new teacher one hour to **explain** it.

Reading Skills and Strategies

ACTIVITY. 14 Guess the meaning of the underlined word(s). Circle the synonym or restatement in each sentence.

1. Some redwood trees are massive. In fact, they are the largest trees in the world.
2. Sandy is fascinated by herpetology, but I think the study of snakes is creepy.
3. Her knapsack was in the trunk of the car. I know because I put all of the backpacks there.
4. Mrs. Wilson said he was in big trouble. In other words, she said he was going to flunk the class.

ACTIVITY. 15 Guess the meaning of the underlined word(s). Circle the antonym in each sentence.

1. She continued on blithely, but the rest of us were very unhappy.
2. The teacher thinks that Fred is an imbecile. However, I know that he is the smartest student in the class.
3. The Romans liked arches in their designs, but I prefer straight lines to half circles.
4. Some unfamiliar words in a text are insignificant; others are very important.

ACTIVITY. 16 Guess the meaning of the underlined word(s). Circle the synonym, antonym, or restatement in each sentence.

1. Jenny got another kachina for Christmas. She now has three Hopi Indian dolls.

   kachina– _____

2. Plankton, the main food of most whales, used to abound in polar seas in the summer.

   plankton– _____

3. By the 19th century, women had won some freedom. However, few of them took advantage of their emancipation.

   emancipation– _____

4. Her business was successful at first, but it ultimately failed.

   ultimately– _____

5. Many birds migrate in the winter, but starlings stay north all year long.

   migrate– _____

6. Jesse doesn't understand the enormity of this predicament. When he realizes the size of the problem, he is going to be very upset.

   enormity of this predicament– _____

7. California is the most populous state, while North Dakota has the smallest number of people.

   populous– _____

8. Last year, Murray lived in a cramped one-room apartment. Now, he lives in a capacious home on the beach.

   capacious– _____

9. Many defenseless animals look like poisonous or dangerous ones. This device—mimicry—scares other animals.

   mimicry– _____

10. Bears sleep through most of the winter. They eat and drink nothing during their hibernation.

    hibernation– _____

11. Inflation was terrible in Germany after World War I. In fact, in 1923, prices of goods rose unbelievably high, to more than 1,422,900,000 times their pre-war level.

    inflation– _____

12. On October 29, 1929, prices on the New York Stock Exchange plummeted. The price of stock has never fallen so quickly since that day.

    plummeted– _____

13. Fields where animals graze usually do not contain many wildflowers. The animals eat the plants before they can produce flowers.

    graze– _____

14. It took people thousands of years to make instruments to find direction, but birds have these devices built in.

    devices– _____

15. The English navigator James Cook discovered Hawaii. In other words, he found paradise on earth.

    Hawaii– _____

Reading: Fire!

2?

Getting Started

Discuss these questions in pairs or small groups. Share your ideas with the class.

1. Look at the chapter title and the photo. What is this chapter about?
2. Have you ever seen a fire? What was on fire?
3. What are some ways to put out fires?

Strategies Reminder

Comprehension Strategies

Prepare
- Making Predictions about the Text
- Exploring What You Already Know
- Asking Questions about the Text

Read
- Marking the Text
- Reading More than Once
- Using Connectors (I, you, he, she, it, we, they) to Follow Ideas
- Using Signal Words to Predict Ideas

Remember
- Using Pictures

Vocabulary Strategies
- Deciding Which Words Are Important
- Looking for Internal Definitions
- Using Synonyms, Antonyms, and Restatements

1. READING

Prepare

Work with a partner to answer these questions. Explain your answers to the class.

1. Look at the title and the drawing. This reading is probably about _____.

    a. math and fire
    b. things necessary for fire
    c. fire

2. Brainstorm *fire*. List some words connected to the topic.
3. What will you learn about fire? Ask the text a question. Write it down to remember it.

Read

Read the text to get a general idea of the meaning. Don't try to figure out unfamiliar terms. As you read, think of the question you wrote in number 3 of the *Prepare* section. Mark key words and sections as you read.

The Elements of Fire

The Fire Triangle

Three things are necessary for fires—oxygen, fuel, and heat. Oxygen is a common gas. Fuel is any burnable material. For example, paper and wood are fuels because they can burn. However, water is not a fuel because it cannot. The amount of heat necessary is different for each kind of fuel. Wood burns at 617 degrees F, and paper burns at 451 degrees F.

Oxygen, fuel, and heat form the "fire triangle." Every triangle has three sides. If you take away one of the sides, there is no triangle. This is also true for fire. Take away oxygen, heat, or fuel, and there is no fire.

You can use the fire triangle to put out fires. You can put water on a fire to reduce or lower the temperature. You can also take away the fuel. When there is no more fuel, the fire will go out. Another way to put out fires is to remove oxygen. If you put a glass over a candle, the fire uses up the oxygen and then goes out.

Firefighters use the fire triangle to put out fires. They use water, take away burnable material, and they use chemicals to cover a fire. They know that if they take away oxygen, fuel, or heat, the "sides" of the triangle, there will be no fire.

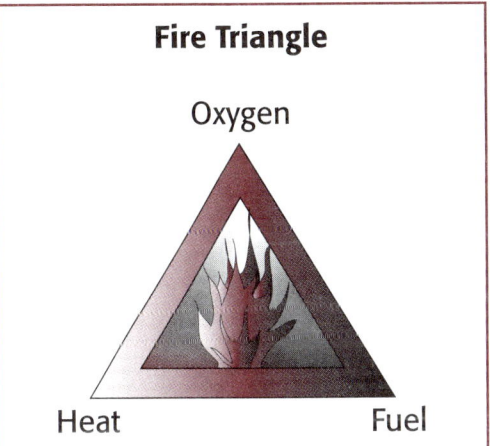

Fire Triangle

Oxygen

Heat   Fuel

Read Again

Read the text a second time. As you read,

- try to understand the "big picture."
- think of more questions and read to find the answers.
- underline key facts.
- try to figure out the meaning of important unknown terms.

Read the text a third time. As you read,

- use connectors to follow ideas.
- use signal words to help you predict ideas.
- pay more attention to parts that confuse you.

Post-Reading Activities

A. Comprehension Check

Mark each statement true (T), false (F), or not in reading (N).

1. _____ All fuels burn at the same temperature.

2. _____ Fuel, heat, and oxygen are necessary to have a fire.

3. _____ To put out a fire, you must remove two sides of the fire triangle.

4. _____ Large fires are easier to control than small ones.

5. _____ Gasoline is not a fuel.

6. _____ Water reduces the temperature of a fire.

B. Vocabulary Check

Work with a partner to answer these questions.

1. Choose the correct two-word verb from the reading to complete each sentence.

   go out   put out   take away   use up

   a. You can _____ a fire with water.

   b. Fires _____ when firefighters _____ all the fuel.

   c. Don't _____ the matches. I need them.

2. Complete the chart for these words from the reading.

Word	Do I know this word?	Is it important?	Is there an internal definition?	Is there an illustration?	Can I guess or should I look in a dictionary?	Meaning
1. oxygen						
2. fuel						
3. amount						
4. triangle						
5. reduce						
6. material						

What other words did you not know? If they are important to the main idea, list them here:

_____

C. Following Ideas

Draw arrows from the underlined pronouns to their referents.

1. For example, paper and wood are fuels because they can burn. However, water is not a fuel because it cannot.

2. Firefighters use the fire triangle to put out fires. They use water, take away burnable material, and they use chemicals to cover a fire. They know that if they take away oxygen, fuel, or heat, the "sides" of the triangle, there will be no fire.

Remember

Use picture notes to illustrate the key points of paragraph 3 in the reading.

Discuss

1. What are some materials that burn easily? Explain how you can put out the fires.
2. What are some materials that do not burn? Name some products that use these materials.

2 READING

Prepare

Work with a partner to answer these questions. Explain your answers to the class.

1. Look at the titles and illustration. This reading is probably about:
   a. wildfires
   b. how to fight wildfires
   c. controlling fire

2. Brainstorm *wildfires*. What are some terms connected to wildfires?
3. What will you learn about fighting wildfires? Ask the text a question.

Read

Read the text to get a general idea of the meaning. Don't try to figure out unfamiliar terms. As you read, think of the question you wrote in number 3 of the *Prepare* section. Mark key words and sections as you read.

Health & Safety

FIGHTING FIRE WITH FIRE

Advances in Fire Fighting

Every year wildfires destroy thousands of acres of forests around the world. How do they start? There are three main causes of wildfires: lightning, accident, and arson. Lightning comes from storms. Accidents happen when people aren't careful with campfires and matches. Arson is a crime. An arsonist is a person who purposely starts a fire.

Whatever the cause, once wildfires start, they are dangerous to people and property. And they are difficult to control. Firefighters say that one of the best ways to fight a wildfire is with fire. They do this with "controlled burns."

What is a controlled burn?

A controlled burn is a fire that firefighters start and control themselves. They use it to destroy the fuel for a fire. The size of the controlled burn varies. It can be small—only 10 or 15 acres, the size of a city block. It can also be very large—thousands of acres, the size of a small town. Of course, firefighters must be careful with controlled burns. The weather has to be exactly right. For example, they don't start them on windy days. In 2001, a controlled burn almost destroyed the city of Los Alamos, New Mexico, because it was too windy.

How do controlled burns stop wildfires?

Controlled burns have two purposes: to prevent a fire from beginning, and to control a fire that is burning. Firefighters use controlled burns to create a "firebreak." What is a firebreak? An area of ground that has no fuel. Roads and rivers are examples of natural firebreaks. Firefighters may burn trees near a house. Or, they may burn several acres of a forest. Either way, fire cannot spread across the firebreak.

Controlled burns are especially effective with wildfires. For example, if a wildfire is burning near a river, firefighters will start a controlled burn nearby. The controlled fire uses up the fuel and creates an even larger firebreak. The raging wildfire cannot spread across the firebreak where all the fuel has been burned away.

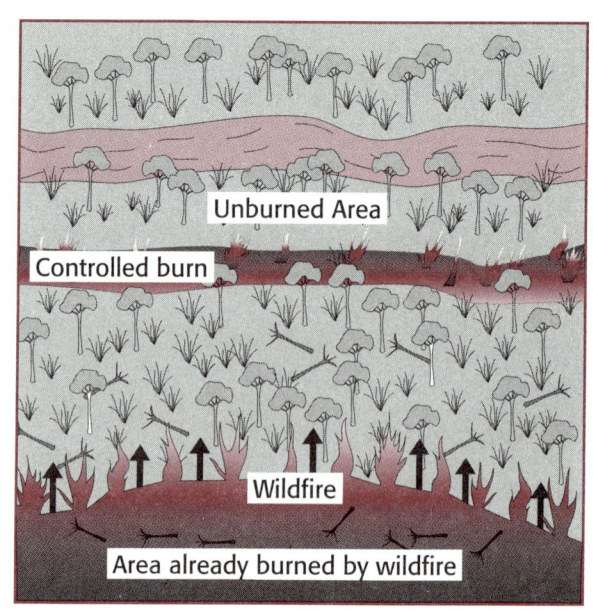

Wildfire Moving Toward a Controlled Burn

Summary

Wildfires destroy millions of dollars' worth of property every year and kill many people. Firefighters use several methods to put them out. However, with modern firefighting techniques such as controlled burns, wildfires will not be as dangerous in the future.

Read Again

Read the text a second time. As you read,

- think of more questions and read to find the answers.
- underline key facts.
- try to figure out the meaning of important unknown terms.

Read the text a third time. As you read,

- use connectors to follow ideas.
- use signal words to help you predict ideas.
- pay more attention to parts that confuse you.

Post-Reading Activities

A. Comprehension Check

Answer these questions about the reading.

1. What natural event may cause a wildfire?
2. How do people start wildfires?

3. How does a controlled burn help control a wildfire?
4. Are controlled burns small fires?
5. Why is weather important for a controlled burn?
6. Do firefighters use controlled burns near homes? Why or why not?

B. Vocabulary Check

Work with a partner to answer these questions.

1. Write the meaning of *arsonist*.

   arsonist _____

2. Compound words are two words combined into one. List three more for *fire*. Define each compound word.

   firefighter   a person who fights fire

   _____   _____

   _____   _____

   _____   _____

3. Complete the chart for these words from the reading.

Word or Phrase	Do I know this word or phrase?	Is it important?	Is there an internal definition?	Is there an illustration?	Can I guess or should I look in a dictionary?	Meaning
1. destroy						
2. acres						
3. forests						
4. lightning						
5. crime						
6. controlled burn						
7. varies						

What other words did you not know? If they are important to the main idea, list them here:

_____

34 CHAPTER 2

C. Following Ideas

Draw arrows from the underlined pronouns to their referents. One pronoun has no referent.

A controlled burn is a fire that firefighters start and control themselves. They use it to destroy the fuel for a fire. The size of the controlled burn varies. It can be small—only 10 or 15 acres, the size of a city block. It can also be very large—thousands of acres, the size of a small town. Of course, firefighters must be careful with controlled burns. The weather has to be exactly right. For example, they don't start them on windy days. In 2001, a controlled burn almost destroyed the city of Los Alamos, New Mexico, because it was too windy.

Remember

Use a picture note to show how a firebreak can stop a fire.

Discuss

1. Have you ever seen a wildfire? Describe it to your class.
2. Where do wildfires happen most in your country? How do they start?

3 READING

Prepare

Work with a partner to answer these questions. Explain your answers to the class.

1. Skim the titles and the first few sentences. Look at the photo. What is the topic?
2. Brainstorm famous city fires. List several words connected to the topic.
3. What will the reading say about the Great Chicago Fire? Ask the text a question.

Read

Read the text to get a general idea of the meaning. Don't try to figure out unfamiliar terms. As you read, think of the question you wrote in number 3 of the *Prepare* section. Mark key words and sections as you read.

It was like a snowstorm, only the flakes were red instead of white.
—Bessie Bradwell Helmer, a survivor of the Great Chicago Fire

THE GREAT CHICAGO FIRE

People say the Great Chicago Fire started in a barn. The date was October 8, 1871. It was a Sunday evening in fall. The autumn trees were dry, and the wind was strong. The city began burning. Wooden streets, sidewalks, and bridges burst into flames. Even the river burned when wooden boats and oil on the water caught fire. No one is really sure how the fire started. Once it did, it destroyed Chicago.

The fire started on the south side of the city and headed toward downtown. Around midnight, the high wind carried it across the Chicago River. By 3:30 A.M., the water pumping station was gone. Without water, the firefighters could not work. Downtown, the fire burned the Palmer House, a beautiful new hotel. It also destroyed the "fireproof" offices of the *Chicago Tribune* newspaper. By noon on Monday, the fire was at the northern edge of the city. Finally, on Tuesday morning, rain began to fall, and the flames finally died out. However, by that time, much of Chicago was in ruins.

In the end, the fire destroyed an area four miles long, and three quarters of a mile wide—more than 2,000 acres. This area included 28 miles of streets, 120 miles of sidewalks, and over 2,000 lampposts. Eighteen thousand buildings were gone, and more than 200 million dollars in property was lost. One hundred thousand Chicagoans lost their homes, and many more lost their jobs.

The Great Chicago Fire destroyed much of the city, but it did not destroy the people of Chicago. They immediately started rebuilding. Just 18 months later, in the spring of 1873, the people of Chicago held a celebration in honor of the rebirth of their city.

Read Again

Read the text a second time. As you read,

- think of more questions and read to find the answers.
- underline key facts.
- try to figure out the meaning of important unknown terms.

Read the text a third time. As you read,

- use connectors to follow ideas.
- use signal words to help you predict ideas.
- pay more attention to parts that confuse you.

Post-Reading Activities

A. Comprehension Check

Answer these questions about the reading.

1. Who started the Great Chicago Fire?
2. Why did the fire spread quickly?
3. When and why did firefighters stop fighting the fire?
4. Approximately how long did the fire burn?
5. What put the fire out?
6. How large was the burned area?
7. How long did it take Chicagoans to rebuild their city?

B. Vocabulary Check

Work with a partner to answer these questions.

1. Underline two phrases in paragraph 1 that mean "started to burn."
2. Complete the chart for these words from the reading.

Word or Phrase	Do I know this word or phrase?	Is it important?	Is there an internal definition?	Is there an illustration?	Can I guess or should I look in a dictionary?	Meaning
1. headed						
2. water pumping station						
3. fireproof						
4. died out						
5. in ruins						
6. rebuilding						
7. celebration						
8. rebirth						

What other words did you not know? If they are important to the main idea, list them here:

_____

C. Following Ideas

1. Draw arrows from the underlined pronoun phrases to their referents.

    By noon on Monday, the fire was at the northern edge of the city. Finally, on Tuesday morning, rain began to fall, and the flames finally died out. However, by that time, much of Chicago was in ruins.
    In the end, the fire destroyed an area four miles long, and three quarters of a mile wide—more than 2,000 acres. This area included 28 miles of streets, …

2. There are three *it* pronouns in paragraph 1 of the reading. Find and underline their referents.

D. Predicting Ideas with Signal Words

1. Scan the reading for these signal words and circle them.
    a. *around*
    b. *by*

c. *by the time*

d. *finally*

e. *in the end*

2. What **kind** of information does each signal word predict?

   a. *around* _____

   b. *by* _____

   c. *by the time* _____

   d. *finally* _____

   e. *in the end* _____

3. What **ideas** does each signal word connect?

   a. *around* _____

   b. *by* _____

   c. *by the time* _____

   d. *finally* _____

   e. *in the end* _____

Remember

Draw a simple map for the Great Chicago Fire. Show where it started and the places it destroyed.

Discuss

1. Why did the Great Chicago Fire spread so quickly?
2. Could a fire like this happen today? Why or why not?

4. READING

Prepare

Work with a partner to answer these questions. Explain your answers to the class.

1. What are coal fires? Which strategy can help you decide the topic?
2. Brainstorm *coal* and *fires*. Compare your list of words with another pair's.
3. What will you learn about coal fires? Ask the text a question.

Read

Read the text to get a general idea of the meaning. Don't try to figure out unfamiliar terms. As you read, think of the question you wrote in number 3 of the *Prepare* section. Mark key words and sections as you read.

Keeping an Eye on Coal Fires

CRAIG, CO—Near Craig, Colorado, a fire is burning. It started more than 50 years ago. Its temperature is more than 1,100 degrees F. This fire may be huge, but no one has ever seen it. That's because it's burning 65 feet underground, in an old coalmine.

Satellites above the earth may help scientists fight underground coal fires like the one in Colorado. These fires sometimes start from natural causes such as lightning. They also start when people burn garbage in old mines. The fires keep burning because they have fuel, oxygen, and heat. Anupma Prakash, a geologist with the International Institute for Aerospace Survey and Earth Sciences in the Netherlands, is studying the problem. He says that it is important to put out the fires when they are still small.

When they get too big, coal fires are impossible to put out. They may burn for years and years. Experts believe that Australia's Burning Mountain started burning about 2,000 years ago. A mine fire in India began in 1916, and is still burning. Coal fires sometimes cause residents to move. The people of Centralia, Pennsylvania tried to put out a coal fire for 20 years. In 1983, they finally voted to leave their town. Coal fires also cause pollution. In one year, underground coal fires in China cause more air pollution than all the cars and trucks in the United States.

Scientists such as Anupma Prakash hope that in the future, coal fires will be found and put out before they grow too big to control.

Read Again

Read the text a second time. As you read,

- try to understand the "big picture."
- think of more questions and read to find the answers.
- try to figure out the meaning of important unknown terms.

Read the text a third time. As you read,

- use connectors to follow ideas.
- pay more attention to parts that confuse you.

Post-Reading Activities

A. Comprehension Check

Answer these questions about the reading.

1. What is unusual about the fire in Colorado?
2. How will satellites help fight these fires?

3. How do these fires start?
4. Why are these fires difficult to control?
5. What problems do these fires cause?

B. Vocabulary Check

Work with a partner to answer these questions.

1. Which words are **not** important to the main idea of the following sentence? Why? Share your opinions with the class.

    Anupma Prakash, a geologist with the International Institute for Aerospace Survey and Earth Sciences in the Netherlands, is studying the problem.

    _____

    _____

2. Complete the chart for these words from the reading.

Word	Do I know this word?	Is it important?	Is there an internal definition?	Can I guess or should I look in a dictionary?	Meaning
1. huge					
2. underground					
3. satellites					
4. garbage					
5. geologist					
6. residents					

What other words did you not know? If they are important to the main idea, list them here:

_____

C. Following Ideas

Draw arrows from the underlined pronouns to their referents.

1. This fire may be huge, but no one has ever seen it. That's because it's burning 65 feet underground, in an old coalmine.
2. Satellites above the earth may help scientists fight underground coal fires like the one in Colorado. These fires sometimes start from natural causes such as lightning. They also start when people burn garbage in old mines.

3. The fires keep burning because they have fuel, oxygen, and heat. Anupma Prakash, a geologist with the International Institute for Aerospace Survey and Earth Sciences in the Netherlands, is studying the problem. He says that it is important to put out the fires when they are still small.

4. When they get too big, coal fires are impossible to put out. They may burn for years and years. Experts believe that Australia's Burning Mountain started burning about 2,000 years ago.

5. The people of Centralia, Pennsylvania, tried to put out a coal fire for 20 years. In 1983, they finally voted to leave their town.

Remember

Note the differences between underground coal fires, wildfires, and the Great Chicago Fire. Use the chart or another type of picture note.

Fire	Cause(s)	Time Fire Lasts/Lasted	Kinds of Damage	How Put Out
1. underground coal fires				
2. wildfires				
3. Great Chicago Fire				

Discuss

1. Compare the three fires you noted in the previous step. Look at your notes if necessary.
2. Do you agree or disagree with this statement: "Underground coal fires are not as dangerous as other fires." Give reasons. Do not look at your notes.

Reviewing Your Reading

A. Look at the following list of the readings in this chapter. Check the column that shows how easy or difficult the material was for you.

Name of Reading	Easy	Average	Difficult
1. The Elements of Fire			
2. Fighting Fire with Fire			
3. The Great Chicago Fire			
4. Keeping an Eye on Coal Fires			

B. Read the following list of strategies that you have practiced in this chapter. Review the readings. Check which strategies you used, and how you used them.

Strategy	Always	Often	Sometimes	Never
Prepare				
Making predictions about the text				
Exploring what you already know				
Asking questions about the text				
Read/Read Again				
Marking the text				
Reading more than once				
Using connectors (*I, you, he, she, it, we, they*) to follow ideas				
Using signal words to predict ideas				
Remember				
Using pictures				
Vocabulary Strategies				
Deciding which words are important				
Looking for internal definitions				
Using synonyms, antonyms, and restatements				

Reading: The Extraordinary Shark

Getting Started

Discuss these questions in pairs or small groups. Share your ideas with the class.

1. Look at the chapter title. What will this chapter say about sharks?
2. Look at the photo of the shark. What does a shark look like?
3. Are sharks and shark attacks common in your country? Why or why not?

The Extraordinary Shark 43

Strategies Reminder

Comprehension Strategies
Prepare
- Making Predictions about the Text
- Exploring What You Already Know
- Asking Questions about the Text

Read
- Marking the Text
- Reading More than Once
- Using Connectors *(I, you, he, she, it, we, they)* to Follow Ideas
- Using Signal Words to Predict Ideas

Remember
- Using Pictures

Vocabulary Strategies
- Deciding Which Words Are Important
- Looking for Internal Definitions
- Using Synonyms, Antonyms, and Restatements

1. READING

Prepare

Work with a partner to answer these questions. Explain your answers to the class.

1. The topic of this reading is _____ _____.
    a. key facts about sharks
    b. the danger of sharks
    c. sharks and fish

2. Think about fish and sharks. Prepare a list of terms that might be in the text.
3. What will the reading say about sharks? Write your question down to remember it.

Read

Read the text to get a general idea of the meaning. Don't try to figure out unfamiliar terms. As you read, think of the question you wrote in number 3 of the *Prepare* section. Mark key words and sections as you read.

SOME BASIC FACTS ABOUT SHARKS

Everyone knows what sharks look like. We also know that sharks can be dangerous. However, many people may not realize that sharks are one of the oldest species of animals on earth, as well as one of the most interesting.

Sharks share some things in common with other fish, but they are somewhat different. First of all, almost all sharks are carnivores, or meat eaters. They eat dolphins, seals, other sharks, and other fish. Like all fish, though, sharks are cold-blooded animals—their bodies change temperature as the water temperature changes. Also, like other fish, the shark's body has gill slits, or openings that help the shark breathe in the water. However, a shark's skeleton is unusual for a fish. Its bones are tough and flexible. In fact, shark bones feel like a human ear. In addition, a shark's skin is unusual for a fish. Its skin is like armor. It has many sharp spikes or nails to protect it. Consequently, you can hurt yourself by just touching a shark's skin.

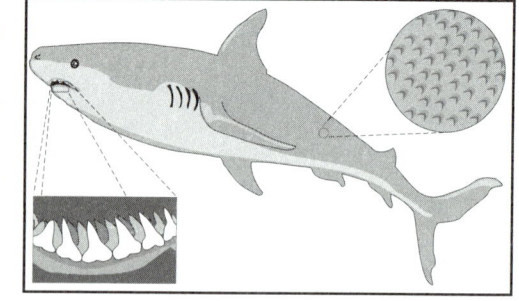

Biologists say that sharks are a very successful species. There are more than 350 different kinds of sharks. They have been around for about 400 million years. That means that they were here before dinosaurs. The dinosaurs are gone, but the sharks live on.

Several things have helped sharks survive. For example, sharks are great hunters. They can hear, smell, and feel everything in the water from long distances. Sharks also have enough sets of teeth for a lifetime. An adult shark uses 7 to 12 sets of teeth in a year. Sharks use their teeth to kill, not to chew. They swallow their food whole or in big pieces.

Another advantage that some sharks have is that they can produce many young at a time. Some sharks lay eggs; others give birth to live babies. Sharks can give birth to as many as 100 pups in one litter. Many sharks do not care for their pups after they are born. After birth, many pups stay close to shore to grow up on their own. A shark is usually not an adult until it is 10 to 15 years old. Some sharks live to be 100.

So the next time you see a frightening picture of a shark, remember that sharks are much more than good killing machines. They are also great survivors.

Read Again

Read the text a second time. As you read,

- think of more questions and read to find the answers.
- underline key facts.
- try to figure out the meaning of important unknown terms.

Read the text a third time. As you read,

- use connectors to follow ideas.
- use signal words to help you predict ideas.
- pay more attention to parts that confuse you.
- check a dictionary for important words that you cannot guess.

Post-Reading Activities

A. Comprehension Check

Answer these questions about the reading.

1. Which animals came first—sharks or dinosaurs?
2. How many kinds of sharks are there?
3. At what age do sharks become adults?

4. Do shark bones break easily? Why or why not?
5. What do sharks use their teeth for?
6. Do sharks live in groups?

B. Vocabulary Check

Work with a partner to answer these questions.

1. Describe a shark's body. Which part is compared to a human ear? Why?

   _____

   _____

2. Complete the chart for these words from the reading.

Word	Do I know this word?	Is it important?	Is there an internal definition?	Is there an illustration?	Can I guess or should I look in a dictionary?	Meaning
1. species						
2. carnivore						
3. cold-blooded						
4. gill slits						
5. armor						
6. spikes						
7. survive						
8. hunter						
9. chew						
10. swallow						
11. pups						
12. litter						
13. survivors						

What other words did you not know? If they are important to the main idea, list them here:

_____

C. Following Ideas

Write the word or phrase each pronoun refers to. If the word does not refer to any word or phrase, put an "X" in the chart.

Pronoun	Line	Refers to
1. they	5	
2. it	11	
3. they	15	
4. they	24	

D. Predicting Ideas with Signal Words

Work with a partner to answer these questions.

1. Scan the reading for these signal words and circle them.

   a. *also*
   b. *consequently*
   c. *first of all*
   d. *however*
   e. *in addition*
   f. *in fact*

2. Find the ideas these words connect. What kind of information does each signal word predict?

   a. *also* _____
   b. *consequently* _____
   c. *first of all* _____
   d. *however* _____
   e. *in addition* _____
   f. *in fact* _____

3. Look at the ideas predicted by *consequently* and *in addition*. Discuss other ideas or information these signal words could predict.

Remember

Draw a picture of a shark. Label the important parts. Look only at the reading while you draw.

Discuss

1. Which do you think are more dangerous—sharks or whales? Why?
2. Why did dinosaurs die out but sharks did not?

2 READING

Prepare

Work with a partner to answer these questions. Explain your answers to the class.

1. Predict the topic of the reading. What strategy will you use?
2. Think about sharks and hunting. What is important when hunting?
3. What will you learn about sharks? Ask the text a question.

Read

Read the text to get a general idea of the meaning. Don't try to figure out unfamiliar terms. As you read, think of the question you wrote in number 3 of the Prepare section. Mark key words and sections as you read.

SHARK SENSE

Sharks are excellent hunters for two reasons. First, their bodies have amazing sensory equipment that helps them find their prey. Sharks can notice even small changes in their environment. Second, sharks are extremely powerful and can easily kill other animals.

FEELING A **shark** can sense weak electricity that small fish create when they breathe.

SEEING Like a cat, a **shark's** eyes are quite sensitive. They can see even when there is very little light. A **shark** must move its head from side to side to see objects directly in front of it.

SMELLING A **shark** has a great sense of smell. It can smell incredibly small amounts of blood in the water—as low as one part per million.

HEARING Sharks have especially sensitive ears. A **shark** can hear sounds 200 yards (550 meters) away. Some sharks can hear sounds up to $1/4$ of a mile (1,100 meters) away.

JAWS A **shark's** jaws are made of cartilage rather than bone. They contain several rows of very sharp teeth. Each time the shark loses a tooth, another moves forward to replace it. A great white shark's jaws are incredibly powerful. They can bite with a pressure of 2,000 lbs. per sq. in. (140 kg/sq cm).

Read Again

Read the text a second time. As you read,

- think of more questions and read to find the answers.
- try to figure out the meaning of important unknown terms.

Read the text a third time. As you read,
- use connectors to follow ideas.
- pay more attention to parts that confuse you.

Post-Reading Activities

A. Comprehension Check

Complete the chart with information from the reading.

Why Sharks Are Great Hunters

Shark Characteristic	Example

B. Vocabulary Check

Work with a partner to answer these questions.

1. Complete the sentences. Choose the correct form of the word *sense*.

    sense   senses   sensing   sensitive   sensory

    a. There are five _____ — taste, touch, sight, hearing, and smell.

    b. Your eyes are an example of _____ equipment.

    c. Sharks have very _____ eyes.

    d. Sharks can _____ other animals from far away.

2. What is a general synonym for **all** of the italicized words? Write it in the blanks.

    a. *extremely*   or _____ powerful

    b. *quite*   or _____ sensitive

c. *incredibly* or _____ small amounts

d. *especially* or _____ sensitive

e. *amazingly* or _____ powerful

3. Complete the chart for these words from the reading.

Word	Do I know this word?	Is it important?	Is there an internal definition?	Can I guess or should I look in a dictionary?	Meaning
1. equipment					
2. prey					
3. environment					
4. weak					
5. jaws					
6. cartilage					
7. sharp					
8. pressure					

What other words did you not know? If they are important to the main idea, list them here:

_____

C. Following Ideas

Write the word or phrase each pronoun refers to. If the word does not refer to any word or phrase, put an "X" in the chart.

Pronoun	Line	Refers to
1. they	5	
2. it	7	
3. it	8	
4. they	13	
5. they	15	

50 CHAPTER 3

Remember

Use a picture note to show a shark's senses. Label it with information from the reading. Compare your drawing with a classmate's.

Discuss

1. Name other animals with amazing senses. Describe the special senses they have.
2. Sharks prey on other fish. What animals prey on sharks?

3. READING

Prepare

This reading is divided into two parts, A and B. Work with a partner to answer these questions based on both parts. Explain your answers to the class.

1. Look at the titles and subtitles. What is the topic of the reading?
2. Why do sharks attack people? Brainstorm reasons. Prepare a list of terms.
3. Part A says there are myths about sharks. What are the myths?

Read Part A

Read the text to get a general idea of the meaning. Don't try to figure out unfamiliar terms. As you read, think of the question stated in number 3 of the *Prepare* section. Mark key words and phrases as you read.

FISH STORIES

This month's column by freelance writer, Sandy Patterson

Are Sharks Really Dangerous to People?

1 Dr. Samuel Gruber, a biologist at the University of Miami's Rosenstiel School of Marine and Atmospheric Science, is a shark expert. In a recent interview with *Science* magazine, Dr. Gruber explained there are many myths, or untrue stories, about sharks. One of these myths is that sharks are very dangerous to people. Why is the danger of sharks to humans a myth? First, 5 many sharks are too small to kill people. In addition, most sharks live in deep water, where people do not swim. According to this expert, sharks only kill about 100 people every year. Elephants kill more than 200 people a year, and dogs kill thousands. Dr. Gruber also claims that people are much more dangerous to sharks than sharks are to people. In fact, people kill up to 100 *million* sharks each year. So although people all over the world are frightened of sharks, it is 10 really sharks who should be afraid of people.

Read Part B

Read the chart. Don't look up unfamiliar terms while reading.

Graphs of Trends in Shark Attacks (1960–2001)
Unprovoked Attacks for World and U.S.A.

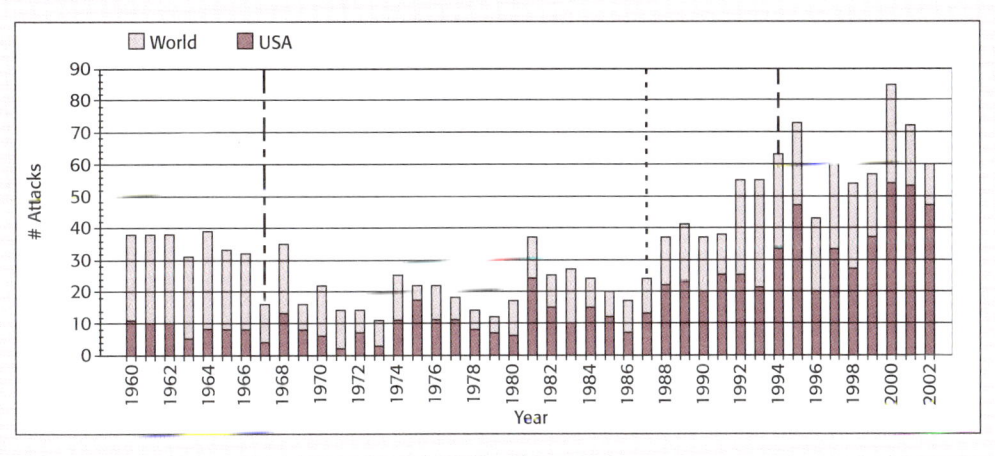

Read Again

Read Part A a second time. As you read,

- think of more questions and read to find the answers.
- try to figure out the meaning of important unknown terms.

Look at Part B a second time. Figure out what the following items represent.

a. black bars _____
b. gray bars   _____
c. horizontal line _____
d. vertical line _____

Post-Reading Activities

A. Comprehension Check

Answer these questions about both parts of the reading.

1. What are two reasons most sharks are not dangerous to people?
2. According to Dr. Gruber, are sharks, dogs, or elephants the most dangerous to people?
3. How many people do sharks kill every year?
4. How many sharks do people kill every year?
5. How many Americans died from shark attacks in 2001?

52 CHAPTER 3

6. How many non-Americans died from shark attacks in 2001?
7. What year had the most shark attacks?

B. Vocabulary Check
Work with a partner to complete the chart for these words from the reading.

Word	Do I know this word?	Is it important?	Is there an internal definition?	Is there an illustration?	Can I guess or should I look in a dictionary?	Meaning
1. Rosenstiel						
2. atmospheric						
3. expert						
4. myth						
5. trends						
6. unprovoked						

What other words did you not know? If they are important to the main idea, list them here:

_____

C. Following Ideas
What does *it* refer to in this sentence?

So although people all over the world are frightened of sharks, it is really sharks who should be afraid of people.

D. Predicting Ideas with Signal Words
Scan Part A for signal words predicting addition. Remember, they tell you that the writer will be adding similar ideas. Compare your list with a classmate's. Include the ideas that the signal words predict.

Remember

Draw a bar graph that shows how many people sharks, dogs, and elephants kill each year.

Discuss

1. Did the information in these readings surprise you? Why or why not?
2. "Fish Stories" is a humorous or casual title for articles about fish. Is this reading humorous or serious? Explain your opinion.

4. READING

Prepare

Work with a partner to answer these questions. Explain your answers to the class.

1. What is this reading about? How do you know?
2. Brainstorm shark attacks and injuries. Exchange ideas with another pair. Then prepare your own list of terms.
3. What will you learn about this shark attack? Ask the text a question.

Read

Read the text to get a general idea of the meaning. Don't try to figure out unfamiliar terms. As you read, think of the question you wrote in number 3 of the *Prepare* section. Mark key words and sections as you read.

Shark Sinks Teeth into Teen

MARATHON, Florida—A shark bit a teenager in the ocean near the Florida Keys this week. After the attack, it was impossible to remove the shark. It remained attached to the boy's chest until doctors removed it at the hospital.

Kevin Morrison, 16, Rockford, Illinois, was scuba diving with his father near Marathon in the Florida Keys. He saw a three foot nurse shark swimming near him, and pulled its tail.

Suddenly, the shark bit Morrison's chest. Rescuers took the boy and the shark to Fisherman's Hospital. Doctors had to operate on the shark to open its jaws. They later took care of the boy and sent him home. The shark died.

The Florida Marine Patrol said nurse sharks swim slowly, and can seem harmless. However, they can be dangerous; swimmers should stay away from them.

Read Again

Read the text a second time. As you read,

- think of more questions and read to find the answers.
- try to figure out the meaning of important unknown terms.

Read the text a third time. As you read,

- use connectors to follow ideas.
- use signal words to help you predict ideas.
- pay more attention to parts that confuse you.
- check a dictionary for important words that you cannot guess.

Post-Reading Activities

A. Comprehension Check

Put the events of the shark attack in order. Number them 1–9.

_____ The boy saw the shark.

_____ The boy grabbed the shark's tail.

_____ The shark bit the boy.

___1___ The boy was scuba diving.

_____ People took the boy to the hospital.

_____ Doctors operated on the shark.

_____ The shark died.

_____ The doctors took care of the boy.

_____ The boy went home.

B. Vocabulary Check

Complete the chart for these words from the reading.

Word	Do I know this word?	Is it important?	Is there an internal definition?	Is there an illustration?	Can I guess or should I look in a dictionary?	Meaning
1. attached						
2. chest						
3. scuba diving						
4. Marathon						
5. operate						
6. harmless						

What other words did you not know? If they are important to the main idea, list them here:

_____

C. Following Ideas

Write the word or phrase each pronoun refers to. If the word does not refer to any word or phrase, put an "X" in the chart.

Pronoun	Line	Refers to
1. it	3	
2. its	9	
3. they	13	
4. they	16	

D. Predicting Ideas with Signal Words

1. Scan the reading for a signal word predicting contrast. Remember, it tells you that the writer will be contrasting a previous idea. What is the word? _____

2. Find the idea that the signal word predicts. Restate the idea in your own words.

_____

_____

Remember

Scan the reading for main events. Mark the key term of each event. Number the events in order. Cover your book, and tell the story to a classmate.

Discuss

1. Did the boy in the story act wisely? Why or why not?
2. Imagine the shark that bit the boy and describe it.

Reviewing Your Reading

A. Look at the following list of the readings in this chapter. Check the column that shows how easy or difficult the material was for you.

Name of Reading	Easy	Average	Difficult
1. Some Basic Facts About Sharks			
2. Shark Sense			
3. Fish Stories			
4. Shark Sinks Teeth into Teen			

B. Read the following list of strategies that you have practiced in this chapter. Review the readings. Check which strategies you used, and how often you used them.

Strategy	Always	Often	Sometimes	Never
Prepare				
Making predictions about the text				
Exploring what you already know				
Asking questions about the text				
Read/Read Again				
Marking the text				
Reading more than once				
Using connectors (*I, you, he, she, it, we, they*) to follow ideas				
Using signal words to predict ideas				
Remember				
Using pictures				
Vocabulary Strategies				
Deciding which words are important				
Looking for internal definitions				
Using synonyms, antonyms, and restatements				

Reading: All About Hair

Getting Started

Discuss these questions in pairs or small groups. Share your ideas with the class.

1. Look at the photo. When and where was this hairstyle popular?
2. Is hair important? Why or why not?
3. This chapter is all about hair. What will the readings say?

Strategies Reminder

Comprehension Strategies

Prepare
- Making Predictions about the Text
- Exploring What You Already Know
- Asking Questions about the Text

Read
- Marking the Text
- Reading More than Once
- Using Connectors *(I, you, he, she, it, we, they)* to Follow Ideas
- Using Signal Words to Predict Ideas

Remember
- Using Pictures

Vocabulary Strategies
- Deciding Which Words Are Important
- Looking for Internal Definitions
- Using Synonyms, Antonyms, and Restatements

1. READING

Prepare

Work with a partner to answer these questions. Explain your answers to the class.

1. This reading is about _____.
   a. hairstyles
   b. changing our hair
   c. why hair is important

2. Brainstorm opinions about hair.
3. The reading says people have strong opinions about hair. Why?

Read

Read the text to get a general idea of the meaning. Don't try to figure out unfamiliar terms. As you read, think of the question stated in number 3 of the *Prepare* section. Mark key words and sections as you read.

The Importance of Hair

1 Some of us are proud of our hair. Some of us hate our hair. Many of us spend a lot of money to improve our hair. If it's long, we cut it. If it's straight, we curl it. If it's curly, we straighten it. If we don't like the color, we dye it. We even think that changing our hair can change our lives. A popular advertisement for hair dye once said, "Blondes have more fun." Many women believed it and dyed their hair.

Reading: All About Hair

4

Getting Started

Discuss these questions in pairs or small groups. Share your ideas with the class.

1. Look at the photo. When and where was this hairstyle popular?
2. Is hair important? Why or why not?
3. This chapter is all about hair. What will the readings say?

Strategies Reminder

Comprehension Strategies

Prepare
- Making Predictions about the Text
- Exploring What You Already Know
- Asking Questions about the Text

Read
- Marking the Text
- Reading More than Once
- Using Connectors *(I, you, he, she, it, we, they)* to Follow Ideas
- Using Signal Words to Predict Ideas

Remember
- Using Pictures

Vocabulary Strategies
- Deciding Which Words Are Important
- Looking for Internal Definitions
- Using Synonyms, Antonyms, and Restatements

1. READING

Prepare

Work with a partner to answer these questions. Explain your answers to the class.

1. This reading is about _____.
   a. hairstyles
   b. changing our hair
   c. why hair is important

2. Brainstorm opinions about hair.
3. The reading says people have strong opinions about hair. Why?

Read

Read the text to get a general idea of the meaning. Don't try to figure out unfamiliar terms. As you read, think of the question stated in number 3 of the *Prepare* section. Mark key words and sections as you read.

The Importance of Hair

1. Some of us are proud of our hair. Some of us hate our hair. Many of us spend a lot of money to improve our hair. If it's long, we cut it. If it's straight, we curl it. If it's curly, we straighten it. If we don't like the color, we dye it. We even think that changing our hair can change our lives. A popular advertisement for hair dye once said, "Blondes have more fun." Many women believed it and dyed their hair.

Because people have such strong opinions about hair, it can be a powerful form of social protest. That is why teenagers often use hairstyles to make themselves look different from other people. In the 1960s, African Americans stopped straightening their hair. They allowed it to grow long and bushy. They called this style an Afro. At the same time, many young men refused to cut their hair. This made some conservative people angry. They thought that men should have short hair. One country even banned male tourists with long hair. Only short-haired men were allowed to visit.

Hair is important not only in social protest but as a religious and professional identity. For example, Sikh men do not cut their hair. They twist it around their heads and cover it with a turban. Male Hasidic Jews have long side curls called peyes. And Rastafarians wear their hair in long braids known as dreadlocks. Sometimes jobs require certain types of hairstyles. For example, in England, lawyers and judges wear a wig in court. And soldiers in most countries must have short hair.

Hair is important to people all over the world. That isn't surprising. It can tell us about a person's attitude, work, religion, or ethnic origin. What does your hair tell the world about you?

Read Again

Read the text a second time. As you read,

- identify the point that each example illustrates.
- think of two more questions and read to find the answers.
- try to figure out the meaning of important unknown terms.
- use the illustrations to help you.

Read the text a third time. As you read,

- use connectors to follow ideas.
- use signal words to help you predict ideas.
- pay more attention to parts that confuse you.

Post-Reading Activities

A. Comprehension Check

Answer these questions about the reading.

1. How do people try to change their hair?
2. Why did many women try to dye their hair blonde?
3. What are some examples of people using hairstyles for social protest?
4. What religious groups can be identified by their hairstyles?
5. What two professions have traditional hairstyles?

B. Vocabulary Check

Work with a partner to answer these questions.

1. Complete the sentences. Use the correct forms of the following words.

    curl　　　curls　　　curly

    a. Peggy really likes _____ hair, so she is going to _____ hers.

    b. We cut the baby's hair, but we saved one of the _____.

    straight　　　straighten

    c. Don't _____ your hair. It looks good the way it is.

    d. Susan has long, _____ hair.

2. *Sikh, Hasidic,* and *Rastafarian* refer to a person's _____.
    a. religion
    b. profession
    c. gender

3. Complete the chart for these words from the reading.

Word	Do I know this word?	Is it important?	Is there an internal definition?	Is there an illustration?	Can I guess or should I look in a dictionary?	Meaning
1. dye						
2. protest						
3. bushy						
4. Afro						
5. banned						
6. identity						
7. peyes						
8. dreadlocks						
9. turban						
10. wig						

What other words did you not know? If they are important to the main idea, list them here:

_____

C. Following Ideas
Write the word or phrase each pronoun refers to. If the word does not refer to any word or phrase, put an "X" in the chart.

Pronoun	Line	Refers to
1. it	2	
2. it	4	
3. it	5	
4. they	9	

Remember

Draw picture notes for hairstyles. Show examples for types mentioned in each paragraph. Include your own hairstyle (paragraph 4). Label each drawing.

Discuss

1. Describe a "traditional" hairstyle in your country. Who wears such hairstyles? Why?
2. Who tries new or unusual hairstyles? Why? Describe these hairstyles.

2 · READING

Prepare

Work with a partner to answer these questions. Explain your answers to the class.

1. Look at the titles and subtitles of the reading. What is the topic of the reading?
2. Brainstorm *hair* and *growth*. Prepare a list of key facts.
3. What will the text say about the growth of hair? Think of two specific questions.

Read

Read the text to get a general idea of the meaning. Don't try to figure out unfamiliar terms. As you read, think of the questions you wrote in number 3 of the *Prepare* section. Mark key words and sections as you read.

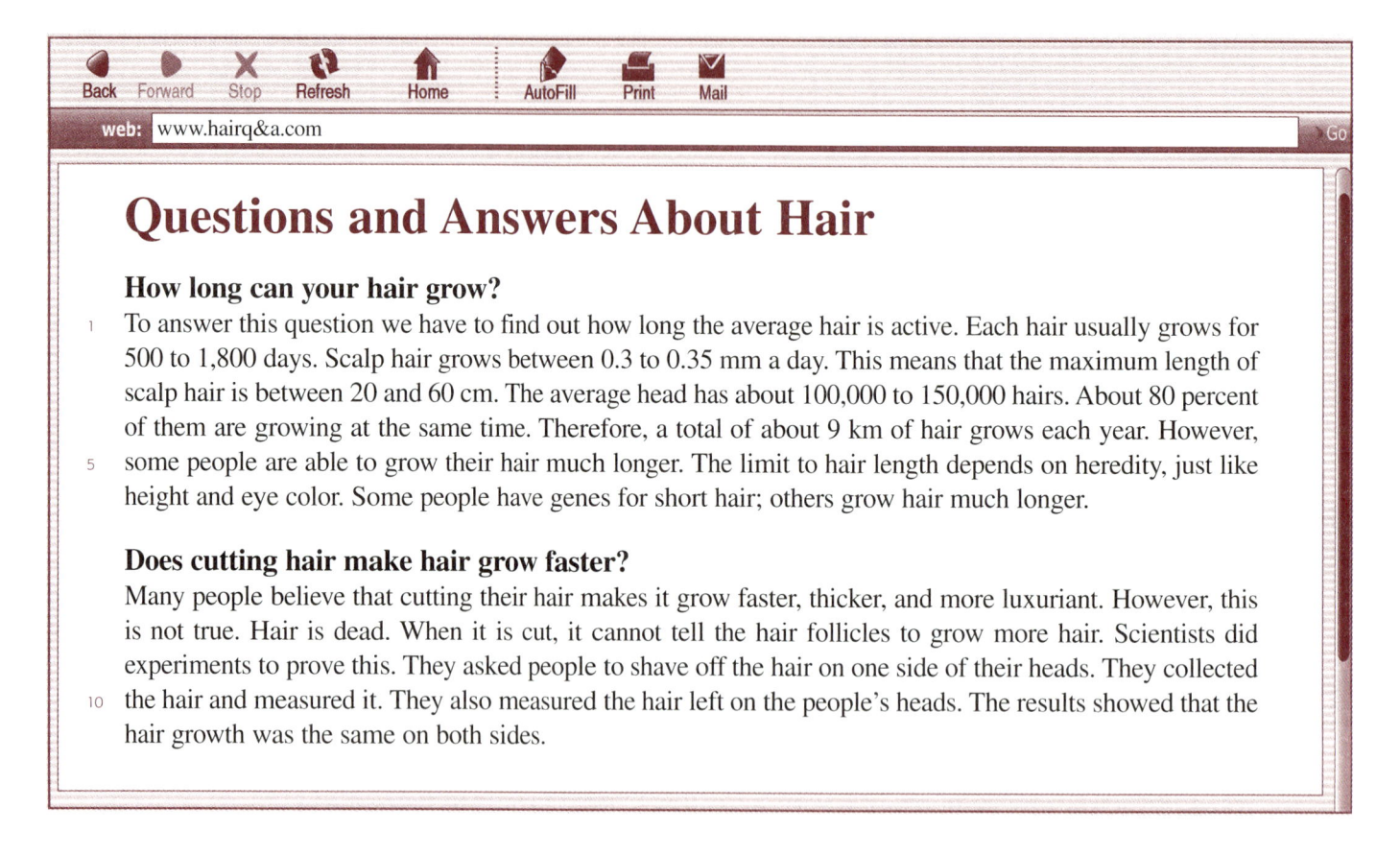

---

web: www.hairq&a.com

Questions and Answers About Hair

How long can your hair grow?

1   To answer this question we have to find out how long the average hair is active. Each hair usually grows for 500 to 1,800 days. Scalp hair grows between 0.3 to 0.35 mm a day. This means that the maximum length of scalp hair is between 20 and 60 cm. The average head has about 100,000 to 150,000 hairs. About 80 percent of them are growing at the same time. Therefore, a total of about 9 km of hair grows each year. However,
5   some people are able to grow their hair much longer. The limit to hair length depends on heredity, just like height and eye color. Some people have genes for short hair; others grow hair much longer.

Does cutting hair make hair grow faster?

Many people believe that cutting their hair makes it grow faster, thicker, and more luxuriant. However, this is not true. Hair is dead. When it is cut, it cannot tell the hair follicles to grow more hair. Scientists did experiments to prove this. They asked people to shave off the hair on one side of their heads. They collected
10 the hair and measured it. They also measured the hair left on the people's heads. The results showed that the hair growth was the same on both sides.

Read Again

Read the text a second time. As you read,

- find and mark the answers to your two questions.
- underline the key sentence in each paragraph.
- try to figure out the meaning of important unknown terms.

Read the text a third time. As you read,

- mark connectors you do not understand.
- use signal words to help you predict ideas.
- pay more attention to parts that confuse you.

All About Hair   63

Post-Reading Activities

A. Comprehension Check

Answer these questions about the reading.

1. Fill in the blanks with the missing information:

   a. Daily growth of scalp hair: 0.3 to _____.

   b. Life of each hair: _____ to _____ days.

   c. _____: 20 to 60 cm.

2. Why do some people have very, very long hair? _____

3. What was the purpose of the experiments? _____

4. What did scientists do in the experiments? Write each step below:

   a. _____

   b. _____

   c. _____

   d. _____

B. Vocabulary Check

Work with a partner. Complete the chart for these words from the reading.

Word or Phrase	Do I know this word or phrase?	Is it important?	Is there an internal definition?	Can I guess or should I look in a dictionary?	Meaning
1. average					
2. scalp					
3. heredity					
4. maximum					
5. genes					
6. luxuriant					
7. follicles					
8. prove					
9. shave off					
10. collected					

What other words did you not know? If they are important to the main idea, list them here:

_____

C. Following Ideas
Write the word or phrase each pronoun refers to. If the word does not refer to any word or phrase, put an "X" in the chart.

Pronoun	Line	Refers to
1. we	1	
2. them	4	
3. it	7	

D. Predicting Ideas with Signal Words
1. Scan the reading for these signal words and circle them.
   a. *however*
   b. *therefore*

2. What kind of information does each signal word predict?

   a. *however* _____

   b. *therefore* _____

3. What ideas does each signal word connect?

   a. *however* _____

   b. *therefore* _____

Remember
Make picture notes that show five facts about hair growth. Label each fact.

Discuss
1. What causes baldness? If you lost your hair, what would you do?
2. What are some products used to make hair grow? Do they work?

3 READING

Prepare

Work with a partner to answer these questions. Explain your answers to the class.

1. What is this reading about? How do you know?
2. Think about foods in your kitchen. Which foods would you use on hair?
3. What will you learn about food and hair care? Think of a wh– question, such as "How will food help my hair?"

Read

Read the text to get a general idea of the meaning. Don't try to figure out unfamiliar terms. As you read, think of the question you wrote in number 3 of the *Prepare* section. Mark key words and sections as you read.

Hair-Care Products from Your Kitchen

Every day, new hair-care products appear in the stores. Many are good but expensive, even though they are made from products you can find in your kitchen. Here are some tips for using these "natural hair-care products." Try them out, and save money.

TO MAKE YOUR HAIR SHINE
Beat an egg and massage it into clean, wet hair. After five minutes, rinse it out with cool water. Do not use hot water, or you will have scrambled egg in your hair!

Mayonnaise is excellent for conditioning hair. Massage it through, and keep it in your hair overnight. Make sure to put a plastic bag on your head, or you will get mayonnaise on your pillow. In the morning, rinse it out carefully in *cool water*. If you use hot water, the mayonnaise will be very difficult to remove. This is good for damaged hair.

Beer also makes hair shine. Rinse your hair in beer in the shower, and then rinse it out with water. Use a beer that does not smell too strong, or people may get the wrong idea.

OILY HAIR
Whenever you wash your hair, put a tablespoon of vinegar in the rinse water. It helps remove the oil, and grease.

DRY HAIR
Olive oil can be a great help for dry hair. Heat half a cup of it. Massage it through your hair. Then wrap your hair in plastic, and cover it with a warm towel. Wait for 30 minutes. Wash the oil out carefully with a shampoo for dry hair.

BLOND HAIR
Lemon juice brightens blond hair. Squeeze two or three lemons into a liter of warm water. Use the water to rinse your hair. Pour it slowly over your hair, massaging it into all of your hair from roots to tips with your fingers. After ten minutes, rinse thoroughly with warm water.

Read Again

Read the text a second time. As you read,

- think of more questions and read to find the answers.
- try to figure out the meaning of important unknown terms.

Read the text a third time. As you read,

- use connectors to follow ideas.
- use signal words to help you predict ideas.
- pay more attention to parts that confuse you.

Post-Reading Activities

A. Comprehension Check

Write the food solution for each problem.

Problem	Solution
1. dry hair	
2. oily hair	
3. hair that doesn't shine	
4. damaged hair	

B. Vocabulary Check

Work with a partner to answer these questions.

1. Homonyms sound the same but have different meanings. Identify the correct meaning of *tips*.

    a. The article gives some <u>tips</u> for using natural hair-care products. _____

    _____

    b. Massage it into your hair from roots to <u>tips</u>. _____

    _____

2. Write the main actions for each tip.

    a. Egg for shine

    1. _____.

    2. _____.

    3. _____.

    4. _____.

b. Olive oil for dry hair

1. _____.
2. _____.
3. _____.
4. _____.
5. _____.

3. Circle the terms that are **not** foods.

massages   mayonnaise   olives   pillows   squeeze   towels

4. Complete the chart for these words from the reading.

Word	Do I know this word?	Is it important?	Is there an internal definition?	Can I guess or should I look in a dictionary?	Meaning
1. conditioning					
2. overnight					
3. shine					
4. oil					
5. grease					
6. brighten					
7. roots					

What other words did you not know? If they are important to the main idea, list them here:

_____

C. Following Ideas

Write the word or phrase each pronoun refers to. If the word does not refer to any word or phrase, put an "X" in the chart.

Pronoun	Line	Refers to
1. it	7	
2. it	25	
3. it	26	
4. it	31	

D. Predicting Ideas with Signal Words

In these sentences, *or* signals an effect. Rewrite each sentence using a different signal word.

1. Do not use hot water, or you will have scrambled egg in your hair!

   _____

2. Make sure to put a plastic bag on your head, or you will get mayonnaise on your pillow.

   _____

3. Use a beer that does not smell too strong, or people may get the wrong idea.

   _____

Remember

Make picture notes for two tips in the reading. Read your partner's notes. Discuss ways to make the ideas clearer.

Discuss

1. Describe hair products your friends use. Are they cheap or expensive? Do they work well?
2. How do you care for your hair? Describe your routines.

4. READING

Prepare

Work with a partner to answer these questions. Explain your answers to the class.

1. What is the topic of this reading?
   a. business empires
   b. a poor person who succeeded in business
   c. the history of African-American businesses

2. The most important question this reading will answer is:

   _____

Read

Read the text to get a general idea of the meaning. Don't try to figure out unfamiliar terms. As you read, think of the question you wrote in number 2 of the *Prepare* section. Mark key words and sections as you read.

Madam C. J. Walker: 19th Century Empress of Hair

How an Uneducated Black Woman Became One of the Wealthiest People in the United States

Madam C. J. Walker was born in 1867. She was an orphan at 7, a wife at 14, a mother at 17, and a widow at 20. She spent much of her early working life as a washerwoman. However, by the time Walker died in 1919, she was one of the wealthiest women in the United States.

Walker's road from poverty to riches began with a dream. At the time, many African Americans lost their hair because they were poor and they didn't eat well. Walker herself had this problem. One night she had an unusual dream. In this dream she received a formula for a special hair cream. With this formula, she developed a product that helped her hair grow. Walker then tried the cream on other people. It worked well on them, too. Soon, she was traveling around the country selling her "Wonderful Hair Grower." Within a few years, hundreds of black women were selling her products, and C. J. Walker was rich.

Developing a cure for baldness may not have been her greatest achievement, however. In addition to employing hundreds of black men and women in her company, she helped thousands of women become successful businesswomen. She opened a school where they could learn the Walker method. After they graduated, her students then used her products in their own hair-care businesses. At a time when most black women worked as maids, cooks, washerwomen, or unskilled factory workers, C. J. Walker had great wealth.

Finally, Walker was also generous to African-American causes. She gave a great deal of money to black colleges and organizations that were fighting for the rights of black people in the United States. Walker was also generous to herself and her daughter. Both women liked spending money. They bought mansions, cars, paintings, clothes, and jewelry. Yet Madam Walker said on her deathbed that her real happiness came from helping her people, an achievement she could look back on with pride.

Read Again

Read the text a second time. As you read,

- think of two more questions and read to find the answers.
- try to figure out the meaning of important unknown terms.

Read the text a third time. As you read,

- mark connectors you do not understand.
- use signal words to help you predict ideas.
- pay more attention to parts that confuse you.

Post-Reading Activities

A. Comprehension Check

Put the events of C. J. Walker's life in order. Number them 1–9.

_____ She tested the hair cream.

_____ She got married.

_____ She started a business.

_____ Her husband died.

_____ She had a strange dream.

__1__ Her parents died.

_____ She became very rich.

_____ She made hair cream.

_____ She had a baby.

B. Vocabulary Check

Work with a partner to answer these questions.

1. Define each compound word.

   a. businesswomen _____

   b. deathbed _____

   c. washerwoman _____

2. Complete the chart with the related words from the reading.

Adjective	Noun
1.	poverty
2. rich	
3.	wealth

3. Complete the chart for these words from the reading.

Word	Do I know this word?	Is it important?	Is there an internal definition?	Can I guess or should I look in a dictionary?	Meaning
1. orphan					
2. widow					
3. formula					
4. cream					
5. achievement					
6. unskilled					
7. generous					
8. causes					
9. a great deal of					
10. mansions					

What other words did you not know? If they are important to the main idea, list them here:

_____

C. Predicting Ideas with Signal Words

1. Scan the reading for these signal words and circle them.
    a. *finally*
    b. *however*
    c. *in addition*

2. Find the ideas that the signal words connect. Restate them in your own words. Compare your answers with a partner's.

Remember

Skim Madam Walker's story, and mark important dates. Draw a simple timeline of the major events of her life.

Discuss

1. Who are today's successful entrepreneurs? How did they make money?
2. Name some companies that failed. Why do you think they failed?

CHAPTER 4

Reviewing Your Reading

A. Read the following list of the readings in this chapter. Check the column that shows how easy or difficult the material was for you.

Name of Reading	Easy	Average	Difficult
1. The Importance of Hair			
2. Questions and Answers about Hair			
3. Hair-Care Products from Your Kitchen			
4. Madam C. J. Walker: 19th Century Empress of Hair			

B. Read the following list of strategies that you have practiced in this chapter. Review the readings. Check which strategies you used, and how often you used them.

Strategy	Always	Often	Sometimes	Never
Prepare				
Making predictions about the text				
Exploring what you already know				
Asking questions about the text				
Read/Read Again				
Marking the text				
Reading more than once				
Using connectors (I, you, he, she, it, we, they) to follow ideas				
Using signal words to predict ideas				
Remember				
Using pictures				
Vocabulary Strategies				
Deciding which words are important				
Looking for internal definitions				
Using synonyms, antonyms, and restatements				

Reading Skills and Strategies

Overview of the Strategies

PART 1

Comprehension Strategies

Prepare
- Making Predictions about the Text

Read
- Identifying the Main Idea
- Using Connectors (Demonstrative Pronouns) to Follow Ideas
- More Practice Using Signal Words to Predict Ideas

Remember
- Using Graphic Organizers

PART 2

Vocabulary Strategies
- Using Grammar
- Using Word Forms
- Using World Knowledge

PART 1 COMPREHENSION STRATEGIES

Prepare

Making Predictions about the Text

The more you predict about a text, the easier it is to read. Titles and illustrations help you guess topics. Other features help you guess much more.

Understanding the Strategy

All features of a text reveal basic or background information. Use the features as clues to help you predict who the text is written for (audience) and what type of text it is (genre). The features also help you predict why it was written (purpose), what it contains (content), and what it is like to read (difficulty).

Use the features to guess basic information about the text.

Features (introduced in Chapter 1)
- title(s)
- pictures, photos, and charts
- length of the text
- name and title or position of the author
- general style (order or appearance of information)
- vocabulary and language (technical or general; short phrases or long explanations)

Basic information the features reveal

Predictions about:	Examples
audience	experts, learners, adults, teens, children, groups with certain interests
genre	newspaper, magazine, textbook, brochure, pamphlet, report, Website
purpose	inform, describe, persuade, give directions or instructions
content type	mostly facts, opinions, descriptions, or explanations
difficulty	easy, average, or hard to read

Example 1

Florida—A Tourist's Paradise

If you want a great vacation, try the sunshine state!
- Luxurious resorts
- Deep-sea fishing
- Disneyworld
- Sea World

Features: short phrases in list, facts and descriptions, title about Florida

Predictions:

Audience: tourists, someone choosing a place for vacation
Genre: brochure
Purpose: persuade, get people to come to Florida
Content: facts and descriptions of Florida
Difficulty: easy to understand

Example 2

Antarctic Ice Sheet Melting

WASHINGTON—A large Antarctic ice sheet is melting and could be gone in 7,000 years, possibly raising worldwide sea levels by 4.8 meters, according to a new study.

Features: place name first in capital letters, long sentences with facts, title about ice melting

Predictions:

Audience: general adult reader (no author's name; a scientist probably did not write the article, so it isn't for experts)
Genre: newspaper
Purpose: inform, give the news about ice sheet melting
Content: facts
Difficulty: could be difficult

ACTIVITY 1 Work in groups. Name the features and make predictions about the text.

Low-Density Lipoprotein and Heart Disease
Sandra Graham, M.D.

Researchers have found that the two main cholesterol-carrying chemicals—low-density lipoprotein (LDL), popularly known as "bad cholesterol," and high-density lipoprotein (HDL), known as "good cholesterol"—have very different effects on the risk of coronary heart disease. Increasing the ratio of LDL to HDL in the blood raises the risk, whereas decreasing the ratio lowers it. By the early 1990s, controlled feeding studies had shown that when a person replaces calories from saturated fat with an equal amount of calories from carbohydrates, the levels of LDL and total cholesterol fall, but the level of HDL also falls. Because the ratio of LDL to HDL does not change, there is only a small reduction in the person's risk of heart disease. Moreover, the switch to carbohydrates boosts the blood levels of triglycerides, the component molecules of fat, probably because of effects on the body's endocrine system. High triglyceride levels are also associated with a high risk of heart disease.

Features: _____

Predictions:

Content: _____
Genre: _____
Purpose: _____
Audience: _____
Difficulty: _____

ACTIVITY 2

Work in pairs. Name the features verbally. Then write predictions about the texts.

1

Britain Tries to Save the Basking Shark

Sandra Kaufman, environment correspondent
Friday November 8, 2002

Britain is going to have new laws. . . .

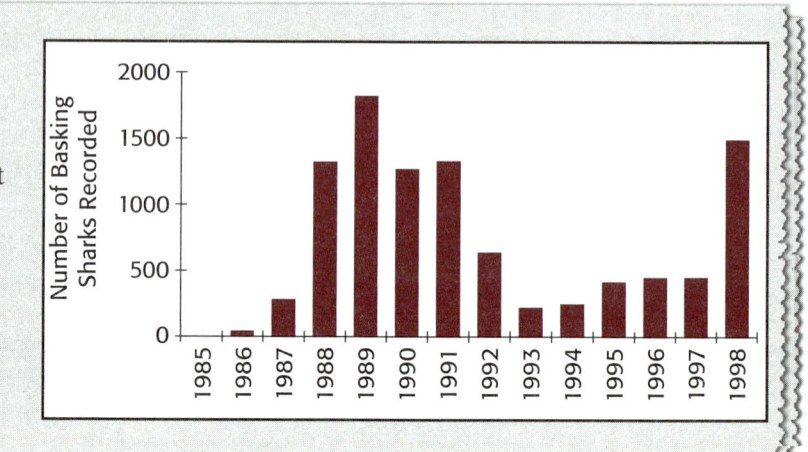

Predictions:
Genre: _____
Audience: _____
Content: _____
Difficulty: _____

2

Save the Basking Shark!

Did you know that giant sharks swim in the waters around Britain? It's true! Britain has the largest number of basking sharks in the world. But don't panic. These sharks live on seaweed, not people! Unfortunately, the basking shark is in trouble.

Predictions:
Content: _____
Difficulty: _____
Audience: _____

3

BASKING SHARK

Order — Lamniformes
Family — Cetorhinidae
Genus — Cetorhinus
Species — maximus

Taxonomy

Occasionally known as "sunfish" or "sailfish" in certain areas of the world, the basking shark is the only member of the family Cetorhinidae. It was first described by Gunnerus in 1765 from a specimen from Norway and was originally assigned the name *Squalus maximus*. Synonymous names include *Halsydrus pontoppidani, Tetroras angiova, Sqalus (Cetorhinus) gunneri, Squalus isodus, Squalus elephas, Squalus rashleighanus, Squalus rhinoceros, Sqalus cetaceus, Cetorhinus blainvillei, Selachus pennantii, Cetorhinus maximus forma infanuncula* and *Cetorhinus maximus normani*. Other scientific names that may be still in use are *Halsydrus maximus, Halsydrus maccoyi, Cetorhinus rostratus,* and *Cetorhinus normani*

Geographical Distribution

The basking shark is a coastal-pelagic species found throughout the world's arctic and temperate waters. In the western Atlantic, it ranges from Newfoundland to Florida and southern Brazil to Argentina, and from Iceland and Norway to Senegal, including the parts of the Mediterranean in the eastern Atlantic. It is found off Japan, China, and the Koreas as well as western and southern Australia and the coastlines of New Zealand in the western Pacific, and from the Gulf of Alaska to the Gulf of California, and from Ecuador to Chile in the eastern Pacific.

Predictions:

Genre: _____

Content: _____

Audience: _____

Read

Identifying the Main Idea

To understand a reading, you must grasp its main idea. This is also true for a paragraph. The main idea is not the topic. Instead, it is the point that the author wants to make about the topic.

Understanding the Strategy

Every reading has at least one main idea. Every well-written paragraph also has a main idea. It is usually stated in a **topic sentence.** Details, such as examples, support or explain it. You can often find the main idea by **location.**

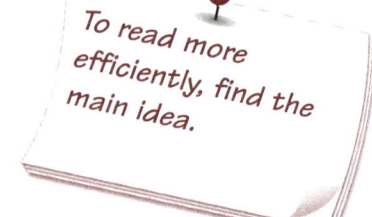

The topic sentence is usually located in three different places in a paragraph:

To read more efficiently, find the main idea.

1. beginning
2. end
3. middle

However, sometimes it is not directly stated:

4. implied

Beginning of the Paragraph

This position is the most common. The topic sentence is the first sentence or one of the first few sentences.

        Main Idea   Supporting Details

Four kinds of mammals live in the sea. The sea otter lives along the shores of western North America and very rarely comes on land. Seals spend most of their lives at sea, but they come on land to have their babies. Whales and sea cows spend their whole lives in the water. They never leave it even to breed.

End of the Paragraph

The topic sentence is the last sentence, or near the end of the paragraph.

                     Supporting Details

When we stand in open country where there are no mountains and buildings to block our view, the earth looks flat to us. We have the feeling that, if we walked far enough in any direction, we could easily come to the ends of the earth. It is no wonder, then, that **even after Columbus proved the earth is round, the myth that we could fall off the edge persisted.**

                     Main Idea

Middle of the Paragraph

The topic sentence can be in the middle. This is common when comparing or listing.

Supporting Details

⟶ Make a realistic budget and stick to it. Leave extra money and credit cards at home when you go shopping. **There are also other useful suggestions for saving money.** Put at least 10 percent of your paycheck in your savings account, and look for ways to cut back expenses.

Main Idea

Implied in the Paragraph

There is not a topic sentence. This is often used for "dramatic effect."

Imagine that you are in an airplane flying 200 miles an hour. If you flew all day and all night without stopping, it would still take you more than 53 years to reach the sun. If you are 15 years old now, you would be more than 68 years old by the end of the trip. Your hair, no doubt, would have turned gray.

The main idea is that the sun is far from Earth. The story, or situation, dramatizes this point.

ACTIVITY 3   Read each paragraph. Underline the main idea.

1. People who live in modern houses have many important services that they do not even think about. They know, for example, that the light will come on when they press an electric switch, and that they can get water by turning a tap. Without these services, life would not be as comfortable. Few people realize what makes these services possible.

2. There are always more animals at the bottom of the food chain than at the top. There are, for example, more insects than frogs, and more frogs than snakes. The animals that are hunted for food are called *prey*, and the animals that eat them are called *predators*. If there isn't enough prey, the predators do not have enough food and they die. When there are fewer predators, the prey has a chance to reproduce more. When there is enough prey, the predators have more food and they are also able to reproduce more. This latter state is called the balance of nature.

3. Today, 2,000 years later, some of these roads still exist. The Romans were the first great road builders in Europe. How did they do it? Their roads were straight and long, and they had several layers. First the builders put down layers of small stones called *gravel*. Then they put large flat stones on top of the gravel. They also made ditches to carry the rainwater away.

4. This suggests another thought about our values. To call them "Italian" does not mean that all Italians think about them in exactly the same way. We disagree among ourselves about many of these values. Each of us must decide how to use them in our lives. We are all Italians whether we always agree or not.

Using Connectors to Follow Ideas

You should remember from Chapter 1 that personal pronouns are connectors. Connectors help you follow ideas through a text. Other parts of speech can also connect ideas.

Understanding the Strategy

Demonstrative adjectives

This, that, these, and those are demonstrative adjectives. However, they can also act in place of nouns. As pronouns, they can refer to a noun or a phrase. The noun or phrase may be a thing, an idea, a person, a situation, an action or event, or a period of time.

Look for this, that, these, those, there, and one to help you follow ideas.

I lived in Chicago from **1993 to 1996,** and those were the happiest years of my life.

She forgot to say thank you, and that was a big mistake.

Adverbs

Adverbs can also act like pronouns. *There* refers to a place, and *then* refers to a time.

She invited us to go on **Wednesday,** but it's not convenient for me to leave then.

We're planning to move to **Florida.** It's always sunny there.

Quantity words

Quantity words can also act like pronouns.

I never had **a bicycle** until my grandfather gave me one for my tenth birthday.

Jim has to read twenty **chapters of the book**. He's reading a few now.

The + noun

The + noun often refers back to a noun. The noun is sometimes renamed.

Mickey ran away. The cat was frightened of a stranger.

Sometimes *there, that,* and *then* do not have antecedents or referents.

He's going to lend me the book **that** I need.
We're going to Paris. **Then** we're going to Rome.
There are twenty-five students in the class.

ACTIVITY 4 Work as a class. Identify the referent for each underlined word.

1. You won the scholarship. That is going to make Dad really happy.
2. My parents want me to go to the state university, but I have decided not to enroll there.
3. You can eat anything you want, but not the eggs. I need those to make the cake.
4. We had lots of fun in class that semester. We were in trouble, but we didn't know it then.

ACTIVITY 5 Draw arrows from the underlined words to their referents. Put an "X" over a word without a referent.

1. Robert's school record was always a good one.
2. Larry gave Phil the money and said, "That's everything that I owe you."
3. Don't walk in the woods at night. There are too many wild animals there.
4. No one knew where John went. That was one reason they were worried.
5. Billy gave his sister a few books for Christmas.
6. I didn't get a license when I first learned to drive. No one needed a license then.
7. The spaceship landed on Mars. There, it started sending messages back to Earth.
8. The giraffe is the strangest animal.
9. "I can't believe that you don't allow pets in the lobby elevator!" Karen said. The building manager explained, "This policy does not mean that we think you are not a good tenant. It's just that we have never allowed pets in the lobby elevator, but you can always take one up in the other elevator."

Using Signal Words to Predict Ideas

Signal words point **to** ideas. However, they also point **back.** They connect effects to causes, solutions to problems, and sequences of events. In this way, they show the order of events, or when things happened. Study the examples below.

Some Types and Examples of More Signal Words

Addition:	*in addition*
Contrast:	*although, instead of*
Effect or Result:	*as a result, therefore, so*
Example:	*for instance*
Listing, Order:	*first, next, then*
Time:	*after, before, then*

Sample sentences

I had many different jobs **before** I became a nurse.
First, I worked as a waitress.
It was hard work, **so** I decided to look for a better job.
Next, I got a job as a cashier in a supermarket. The pay was terrible.
For instance, some weeks, I couldn't even afford to buy gas to go to work.
In addition, the work was really boring.
Then I got a job as a nurse's aide.
Although the work was difficult, I really enjoyed it.
Therefore, I decided to go to nursing school.
As a result, I got a job working for a hospital in town.
After two years, I became the head of my department.

ACTIVITY 6 Use signal words to predict the previous idea. Circle the letter of the correct answer.

1. _____, so their parents bring them food.
   a. Young birds have wings
   b. Young birds cannot fly
   c. Young birds are beautiful

2. _____. For instance, today he's wearing a purple tie with a green shirt.
   a. He often wears strange clothing
   b. He didn't get dressed until noon
   c. He forgot to iron his shirt

3. _____; therefore, we will call her.
   a. Don't wash light and dark clothes together
   b. Stephen was a king of England
   c. We won't have time to visit her

4. _____. As a result, we couldn't make cookies.
   a. Turn the light off
   b. You didn't buy sugar at the grocery store
   c. You remembered the salt

5. _____, although she's never late for work.
   a. The meetings are boring
   b. She never gets to meetings on time
   c. She doesn't wear a watch

6. _____. First, I couldn't pay the tuition.
   a. I enjoyed my classes
   b. Italy is a beautiful country
   c. I had many reasons to quit school

ACTIVITY. 7

Read the paragraph. Note the signal words and the events they connect. Then order the events from 1 to 9.

John got a car before he got his first paycheck. Then he lost his job. As a result, he had to return the car to the dealer. In addition, the dealer made him pay an extra fee for returning the car. Although he was upset at having to return the car, now he's happy. He found a better job. After six months he got a raise, so he bought another car. This time, he got a really good one.

_____ He got a raise.

_____ The dealer made him pay extra money.

_____ He was upset.

_____ He lost his job.

_____ He got a really good car.

_____ He returned the car to the dealer.

_____ He got his first paycheck

__1__ John bought a car.

_____ He found a better job.

Remember

Graphic organizers are another way to picture ideas. They help you memorize key points, but they also help you understand them.

Understanding the Strategy

Different types of texts require different diagrams. A useful diagram shows key points and the connections or relationships between ideas.

Diagram ideas to understand and remember them.

Simple Timeline

Use a **simple timeline** for a text that tells a story across several years.

1865	1885	1890
born	finished school	got married

Block Diagram

Use a **block diagram** to relate events that lead to a final event. This one is for events leading up to a fire.

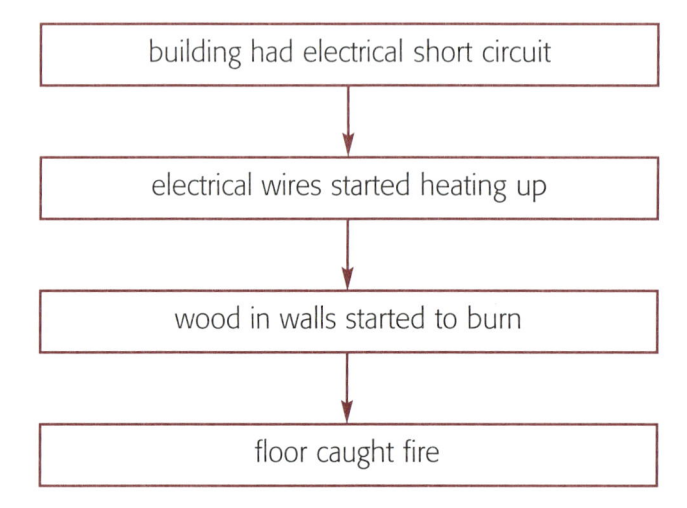

building had electrical short circuit
↓
electrical wires started heating up
↓
wood in walls started to burn
↓
floor caught fire

Flowchart

Use a **flowchart** to show a cycle of events, or events that repeat over and over. This one is the water cycle.

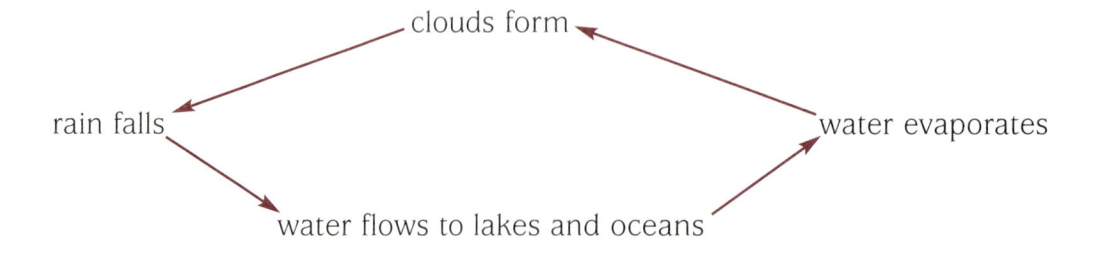

clouds form → water evaporates → water flows to lakes and oceans → rain falls → clouds form

Cluster Diagram

Use a **cluster diagram** for descriptions. This one shows the relationships of different aspects of a wedding.

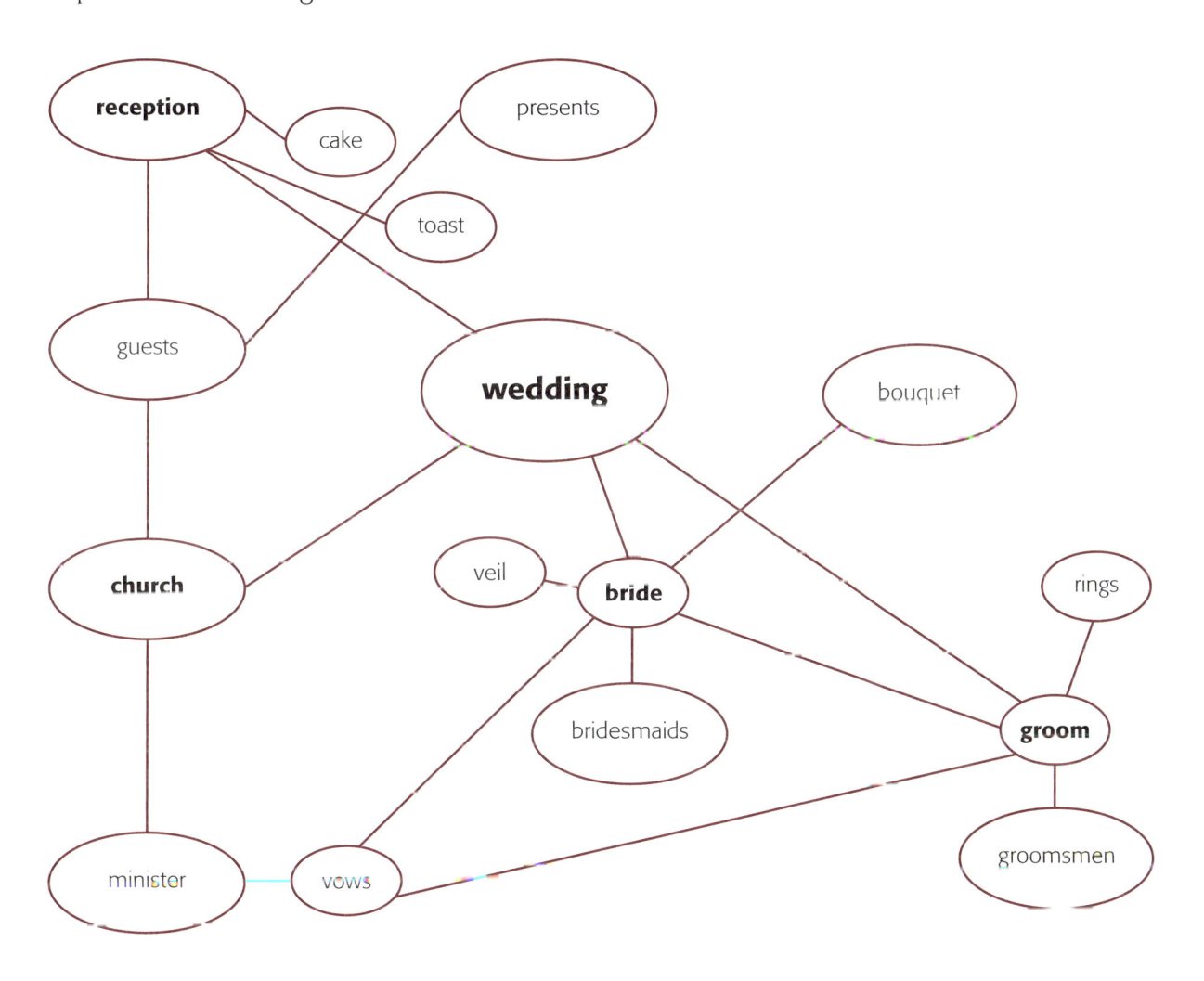

ACTIVITY 8   Choose the best diagram for each topic. Write your answer beside the topic.

1. "The History of the Automobile Industry" _____

2. "The Process of Making Steel" _____

3. "A Description of the Ecosystem in a Rain Forest" _____

4. "Why World War I Began" _____

5. "How Recycling Paper Works" _____

PART 2 · VOCABULARY STRATEGIES

Using Grammar

A text may define new terms, or it may not. Before you check the dictionary, look for other clues to meaning. Grammar is one. Grammar can help you make an educated guess.

Understanding the Strategy

Each part of speech has a different job, or function, within a sentence. It names, describes, or shows the acts of people, places, and things. Learn the job of a new term and you learn a clue to its meaning.

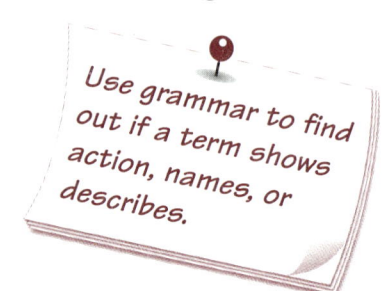

Use grammar to find out if a term shows action, names, or describes.

Nouns

Name a person, place, or thing. They are the subject and object of acts, or the *who* and *what*. They are also the objects of prepositions such as *in, with,* or *by*.

Examples: teacher   Atlanta   history   rain   information

Verbs

Identify acts or states of being. They tell what someone or something *does* or *is*.

Examples: walk   sleep   think   say   feel   is

Adjectives

Describe nouns. They say *which, what kind of,* and *how many*.

Examples: big   red   unusual   European

Adverbs

Describe verbs or adjectives. They say *how* or *how often*.

Examples: happily   frequently   only   enormously   very

Example of guessing meaning from grammar:

David tried to wash the big, yellow armadillo.

What is *armadillo*?

- *Big* and *yellow* describe it > noun.
- It names something big and yellow.
- It's an object of a verb, and tells what David tried to wash.
> *Armadillo* is a thing or an animal. (It is an animal.)

ACTIVITY 9   Use the part of speech to guess the meaning of the underlined words.

1. The repairman used his <u>pliers</u> to open the door.

    what repairman used > noun > names things—a tool?

2. Don and I didn't see each other again until our high school <u>reunion</u> ten years later.

3. She was <u>infinitely</u> more beautiful than her sister.

4. Serena has the best voice in the <u>choir</u>.

5. Mary was so frightened, she became <u>hysterical</u>.

6. My brother and his wife love to eat <u>tandoori</u> bread.

7. The people cheered, and the excitement <u>heightened</u>.

8. <u>Quinine</u> helped his fever, didn't it?

9. Use a <u>shoehorn</u> to put on new shoes.

Using Word Forms

A word form is a different way to identify a part of speech. Some words that are the same part of speech look alike. That is, they have similar forms. A word's form can tell what part of speech it is, and also point to the meaning of the word.

Understanding the Strategy

Form connects words. It helps you relate words you don't know to ones you know. Forms of nouns, verbs, adjectives, and adverbs can be related in two ways: with **prefixes** and with **suffixes.**

Use word form to guess the meaning of a word.

Prefixes

A prefix is a letter or group of letters added to the beginning of a word. A prefix changes a word's meaning. However, it does not change its part of speech. A prefix cannot be used alone or as a suffix.

Example:	adjective	adjective
	happy	**un**happy
	verb	**verb**
	do	**re**do

Suffixes

A suffix is a letter or group of letters added to the end of a word. Most suffixes change a word's part of speech. They always show a shift in meaning.

Example:	verb	noun	adjective
	enjoy	enjoy**ment**	enjoy**able**
	work	work**er**	work**able**

Prefix and Suffix Combinations

Some words combine prefixes and suffixes.

Example: **un**enjoy**able**   **un**happi**ly**

Example of guessing meaning from word forms:

The athlete does 30 repetitions daily of each exercise.

What is *repetitions*?

- "repet" and the suffix "-tion" are basic parts
- "-tion" > noun > names a thing
- "repet" looks like the verb "repeat"
- > *Repetitions* is the action or act of repeating. (Yes, it is.)

ACTIVITY 10

Read the examples. Then use word forms to guess the meaning of the underlined words.

teach	(verb)
reteach	(verb) teach again
teach**er**	(noun) a person who teaches
teach**able**	(adjective) a person who can learn
unteach**able**	(adjective) a person who cannot learn

| wide | (adjective) |
| wid-**en** | (verb) to make something wider |

| hero | (noun) |
| hero-**ic** | (adjective) like a hero |

| home | (noun) |
| home-**less** | (adjective) without a home |

| physics | (noun) |
| physic-**ist** | (noun) a person who works in the area of physics |

| educate | (verb) |
| educa-**tion** | (noun) instruction in schools |

1. I had an accident, and now my car is <u>undriveable</u>.

   undriveable– _____

2. She had to <u>repaint</u> her room because she didn't like the color.

   repaint– _____

3. The news of her death <u>saddened</u> the whole class.

   saddened– _____

4. He had to borrow money because he was <u>penniless</u>.

   penniless– _____

5. The situation is very <u>problematic</u>.

   problematic– _____

6. Don't worry about the cost. The money is <u>unimportant</u>.

   unimportant– _____

7. My uncle is a <u>chemist</u>.

   chemist– _____

8. The <u>builder</u> made many mistakes on our house.

   builder– _____

Using World Knowledge

World knowledge is general knowledge. It's your experience or understanding of how things work, where things are, and who does what in the world. Using it while reading is a powerful strategy for comprehension.

Understanding the Strategy

To use your own knowledge to guess meaning, study the general context of the unfamiliar term. Also, look at specific words you already know or can guess.

Use your general knowledge to guess the meanings of unknown words.

Example of guessing meaning from world knowledge:

A passport is mandatory when you travel overseas.

What is *mandatory*?
- (general context) overseas travel
- (specific words) "passport" = special paper, shows traveler's name and country; "overseas" = over seas = across water
- (your experience and/or knowledge)
  I went to Paris, and I had to have a passport.
  I read about traveling; countries say you *must* show your passport.
- > *Mandatory* means that something is necessary, or that it is a must. (Yes, it does.)

ACTIVITY 11 Use your world knowledge to guess the meaning of the underlined words.

1. Sam failed every class this semester. He is reevaluating his study methods.

   reevaluating– _____

2. The pugilist fought Jackie Chan like a tiger.

   pugilist– _____

3. The two men paddled the Indian canoe gracefully across the water.

   canoe– _____

4. Wolves hunt noisily in packs by day. Cats hunt silently and alone by night.

   packs– _____

5. Outside, the cave was about eight feet across. Inside, the cave narrowed, and there was only room for one person.

   narrowed– _____

6. The child whined to the babysitter that 7:00 was too early to go to bed.

   whined– _____

Reading Skills and Strategies **91**

ACTIVITY 12   Read each paragraph. Decide if each underlined term is important. If it is, use all of the clues and strategies to guess its meaning. Use grammar, word forms, and your world knowledge. If it is not important, simply write "not important" on the line.

1. Any person is likely to look like other members of his family. Size, height, <u>coloring</u>, and even intelligence are <u>handed down</u> from parents to children. However, there are other kinds of family <u>similarities</u>. A child begins to learn as a tiny baby, and his most <u>lasting</u> lessons are learned in the family. He talks like his family talks. He usually enjoys the same kinds of foods that his family likes. He usually believes the same things and has the same values. One of the hardest things in the world to do is to <u>unlearn</u> the lessons learned in your family as a child.

   a. coloring– _____
   b. handed down– _____
   c. similarities– _____
   d. lasting– _____
   e. unlearn– _____

2. The day before the <u>Weston Handicap</u> was gray and cold. Pete rode one race that afternoon, and the cold went through his <u>silks</u> like <u>sleet</u>. After the race, he saw the <u>stable boys</u> running to meet the horses with blankets: warm blankets for the horses, but nothing for the <u>jockeys</u> like him.

   a. Weston Handicap– _____
   b. silks– _____
   c. sleet– _____
   d. stable boys– _____
   e. jockeys– _____

3. One summer afternoon in 1674, <u>Anton van Leeuenhock</u>, the <u>respectable</u> owner of a <u>dry-goods</u> store, went for a ride outside of his hometown of Delft, Holland. Soon he came to a lake. When he got off his horse and <u>approached</u> the lake, he noticed that the water was full of strange, green clouds. He took a <u>vial</u> from his pocket and filled it with the cloudy green stuff.

   a. Anton van Leeuenhock– _____
   b. respectable– _____
   c. dry-goods– _____
   d. approached– _____
   e. vial– _____

Reading: Food on the Run

6

Getting Started

Discuss these questions in pairs or small groups. Share your ideas with the class.

1. Do you eat fast food often? Why or why not?
2. Look at the chapter title. *On the run* can mean "in a hurry" and "in trouble." Scan the titles of the readings. Which readings are about fast-food restaurants in trouble?

Strategies Reminder

Comprehension Strategies

Prepare
- Making Predictions about the Text

Read
- Identifying the Main Idea
- Using Connectors (*this, that, these, those, there, one*) to Follow Ideas
- More Practice Using Signal Words to Predict Ideas

Remember
- Using Graphic Organizers

Vocabulary Strategies
- Using Grammar
- Using Word Forms
- Using World Knowledge

1. READING

Prepare

Work with a partner to answer these questions. Explain your answers to the class.

1. Look at the features of the text. Make predictions about the following items.
   a. topic
   b. content type
   c. audience
   d. difficulty

2. Brainstorm *fast food* and *businesses*. Prepare a list of terms that might be in the text.
3. Ask the text two questions. Write them down to remember them.

Read

Read the text to get a general idea of the meaning. Don't try to figure out unfamiliar terms. As you read, think of the questions you wrote in number 3 of the *Prepare* section. Mark key words and sections as you read.

Name: Jason Wilson, Sophomore

Date: March 12, 2004

Class: Social Studies

The Growth of Fast Food in the United States

Fast food began in the United States fewer than 100 years ago. The first fast-food chain was White Castle. It was started in 1916 by J. Walter Anderson. However, fast food was not an important part of the American diet until after World War II.

In 1948, three years after the end of the war, Richard and Maurice McDonald decided to start a different kind of fast-food restaurant. The brothers had a new idea. They wanted to sell hamburgers cheaply. They hoped to make money by selling inexpensive hamburgers to a lot of people.

To test their plan, the McDonalds opened a hamburger stand in San Bernardino, California. They knew that their restaurant had to be economical and efficient. To make it economical, they reduced costs in several ways. First, their restaurant had no waitresses and no indoor tables. Customers ordered their food at a window and ate in their cars. Then, in order to make their restaurant efficient, they needed to make food more quickly. Therefore, they decided to simplify their menu. They served only a few items—hamburgers, cheeseburgers, french fries, and drinks.

The McDonald's plan worked. In fact, the McDonald restaurant was so successful that the brothers decided to franchise their restaurants. This meant that people would pay the McDonald brothers a fee in order to build restaurants according to the McDonald design. In 1953, franchises opened in Phoenix, Arizona, and Downey, California.

The next step in the growth of McDonald's came in 1954. In that year, a brilliant salesman named Ray Kroc started selling franchises for the McDonald brothers. At the end of 1957, there were 37 McDonald's; by 1959, the total had reached over 100. In 1961, Kroc bought the McDonald Corporation from the two brothers and began building restaurants all over the United States. The success of McDonald's encouraged other people to start fast-food chains. Keith Cramer began a fast-food hamburger restaurant in Miami in 1954. It eventually became Burger King. Dave Thomas opened his first Wendy's restaurant in 1962 in Columbus, Ohio. These businesses became very successful. By 1990, there were 11,803 McDonald's, 6,298 Burger Kings, and 3,721 Wendy's fast-food restaurants in the United States.

Soon, other fast-food chains began selling products such as chicken, pizza, tacos, and submarine sandwiches. Today, 160,000 fast-food restaurants serve more than 50 million Americans daily. With more than $65 billion in sales per year, fast food is one of the most successful American industries.

Read Again

Read the text a second time. As you read,

- think of three more questions and read to find the answers.
- underline the main ideas and circle the dates.
- try to figure out the meaning of important unknown terms.

Read the text a third time. As you read,

- use connectors to follow ideas.
- use signal words to help you predict ideas.
- pay more attention to parts that confuse you.
- think of more strategies to figure out unknown terms.

Post-Reading Activities

A. Comprehension Check

Complete this timeline based on the reading.

Growth of Fast-Food Business in the U.S.

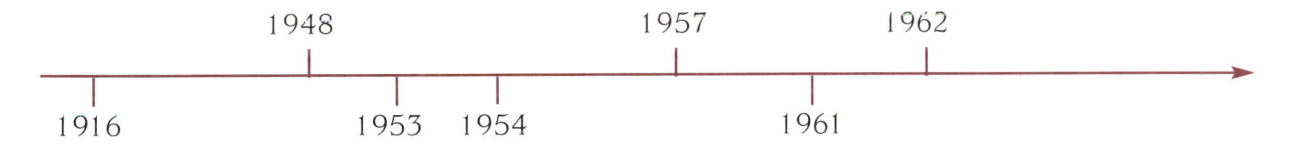

1916 1948 1953 1954 1957 1961 1962

B. Vocabulary Check

Work with a partner. Complete the chart for these words from the reading.

Word	Do I know this word?	Is it important?	Is there an internal definition?	Is it a noun? verb? adjective?	Does it look like a word I know?	Can I use world knowledge?
1. chain						
2. Castle						
3. cheaply						
4. inexpensive						
5. profits						
6. economical						

The "Is it a noun? verb? adjective?" and "Does it look like a word I know?" and "Can I use world knowledge?" columns are grouped under **Other Clues**.

96 CHAPTER 6

Word	Do I know this word?	Is it important?	Is there an internal definition?	Other Clues		
				Is it a noun? verb? adjective?	Does it look like a word I know?	Can I use world knowledge?
7. efficient						
8. simplify						
9. franchise						
10. fee						
11. growth						
12. brilliant						
13. encourage						

What other words did you not know? If they are important to the main idea, list them here:

_____

C. Following Ideas

Write the word or phrase each item refers to. If the item does not refer to any word or phrase, put an "X" in the chart.

Word	Line	Refers to
1. the brothers	5	
2. this	14	
3. there	18	
4. these businesses	22–23	

D. Predicting Ideas with Signal Words

Work with a partner to complete these items.

1. Read each sentence and underline the signal word.
   a. First, their restaurant had no waitresses and no indoor tables.
   b. The next step in the growth of McDonald's came in 1954.
   c. Soon, other fast-food chains began selling products such as chicken, pizza, tacos, and submarine sandwiches.

2. Predict the idea that came **before** each sentence in number 1. Check the reading to see if you are correct.

   a. _____

   b. _____

   c. _____

E. Identifying the Main Idea

Find the main idea in each paragraph of the reading.

paragraph 1 _____

2 _____

3 _____

4 _____

5 _____

6 _____

Remember

Exercise A *(Comprehension Check)* uses one kind of graphic organizer. What is it? Choose another type and use it to chart the following topic.

How to make a profit from an inexpensive product

Discuss

1. How long has your country had fast-food restaurants? Which restaurants do you have?
2. Why did the author of the article write about fast food? Name some other topics about fast food that might interest his audience.

2. READING

Prepare

Work with a partner to answer these questions. Explain your answers to the class.

1. Look at the features of the texts. How is the information ordered?
2. Name a strategy for reading the charts. What information does each chart give?
3. Brainstorm fast-food menus and nutritional terms. Prepare a list of terms.
4. Work alone. Ask two questions about each chart. Write them down. Do not show them to your partner.

98 CHAPTER 6

Read

Scan the charts for the answers to your six questions from number 4 of the *Prepare* section. Write the answers on a separate sheet of paper.

Chart 1

Nutritional Chart for Adult Men and Women

	Calories Max	Fat Max	Cholesterol Max	Sodium Max	Carbohydrate Max	Fiber Min	Protein Max
Women	2,000	65g	300mg	2400mg	300g	25g	50g
Men	2,500	80g	300mg	2400mg	375g	30g	65g

Max = maximum   Min = minimum

Chart 2

Kentucky Fried Chicken

Original Recipe® Chicken								
	Whole Wing		**Breast**		**Drumstick**		**Thigh**	
Serving Size • Grams • Ounces	47 1.6		153 5.4		61 2.2		91 3.2	
Amount Per Serving • Calories • Calories from Fat	140 90		400 220		140 80		250 160	
	Amount	% Daily Value*	Amount	% Daily Value*	Amount	% Daily Value*	Amount	% Daily Value*
Total Fat Saturated Fat	10g 2.5g	15% 12%	24g 6g	38% 31%	9g 2g	13% 10%	18g 4.5g	28% 23%
Cholesterol	55mg	18%	135mg	45%	75mg	25%	95mg	32%
Sodium	414mg	17%	1116mg	47%	422mg	18%	747mg	31%
Total Carbohydrate Dietary Fiber Sugars	5g 0g 0g	2% — —	16g 1g 0g	5% 4% —	4g 0g 0g	1% — —	6g 1g 0g	2% — —
Protein	9g	—	29g	—	13g	—	16g	—
			% Daily Value					
Vitamin A	**	**	**	**				
Vitamin C	**	**	**	**				
Calcium	**	4%	**	2%				
Iron	2%	6%	4%	4%				

Chart 3

McDonald's USA Nutrition Facts

Item	Calories	Calories from fat	Fat (grams)	Cholesterol (mg)	Sodium (mg)	Carbohydrates (grams)	Protein (grams)	Fiber (grams)	Sugars (grams)
Lunch									
Hamburger	280	90	10	30	560	35	12	2	7
Cheeseburger	330	130	14	45	800	35	15	2	7
Big Mac®	580	300	33	85	1050	47	24	3	7
Filet-O-Fish®	470	240	26	50	730	45	15	1	5
Small french fries	210	90	10	0	135	26	3	2	0
Large french fries	540	230	26	0	350	68	8	6	0
Chicken McNuggets® (4)	210	120	13	35	460	12	10	1	0
Chicken McNuggets® (6)	310	180	20	50	680	18	15	2	0
Side salad	15	0	0	0	10	3	1	1	1
Breakfast									
Egg McMuffin®	300	110	12	235	840	29	18	2	3
Sausage biscuit w/egg	490	300	33	245	1010	31	16	1	2
Hash browns	130	70	8	0	330	14	1	1	0
Dessert									
Baked apple pie	260	120	13	0	200	34	3	<1	13
Chocolate chip cookie	170	80	9	5	150	23	2	<1	14
McDonaldland® cookies	230	70	8	0	250	38	3	1	12
Drinks									
1% Lowfat milk	100	20	2.5	10	115	13	8	0	13
Orange juice (16 oz.)	180	0	0	0	5	42	3	0	37
Coca-cola® small (16 oz.)	150	0	0	0	15	40	0	0	40
Coca-cola® medium (21 oz.)	210	0	0	0	20	58	0	0	58
Sprite® small (16 oz.)	150	0	0	0	55	39	0	0	39
Sprite® medium (21 oz.)	210	0	0	0	80	56	0	0	56

Read Again

Exchange questions with your partner. Scan the charts for the answers to his or her six questions. Compare your answers to both sets of questions.

Post-Reading Activities

A. Comprehension Check

Answer these questions about the reading.

1. What is the healthiest meal at a fast-food restaurant? Use the charts to create it.
2. What is the unhealthiest meal at a fast-food restaurant? Use the charts to create it.

B. Vocabulary Check

Work with a partner to answer these questions. Share your opinions with the class. In the reading, there are few clues to the meanings of nutritional terms.

1. Which terms are the most important? Why? _____

   _____

2. Name some ways to guess the meanings of items on the menu. _____

   _____

3. Is the chart useful if you do not know every term? Why or why not? _____

   _____

Remember

You are dieting but want to eat fast food with your friends. Use a graphic organizer to chart items you can eat. Include the nutrition facts for each item.

Discuss

1. Should fast-food restaurants provide nutrition facts? Why or why not?
2. Agree or disagree: People shouldn't eat fast food. Give reasons for your opinion.

3 READING

Prepare

Work with a partner to answer these questions. Explain your answers to the class.

1. The topic of this article is _____.
   a. why Caesar Barber has health problems
   b. a man suing fast-food restaurants because of health problems
   c. a man with health problems

2. This article came from _____.
   a. a textbook
   b. a business report
   c. a newspaper
3. What are the effects of eating fast food? Prepare a list of terms.
4. Ask the text this question: What kinds of health problems did Mr. Barber have?

Read

Read the text to get a general idea of the meaning. Don't try to figure out unfamiliar terms. As you read, think of the question in number 4 of the *Prepare* section. Mark key words and sections as you read.

Man Sues Fast-Food Companies for Health Problems

NEW YORK—A man from New York is suing four big fast-food companies. Caesar Barber is going to court because he says that high-fat foods at McDonald's, Burger King, Wendy's, and KFC Corporation destroyed his health. Barber says that he ate at these restaurants four or five times a week for many years. He claims that this diet made him very overweight. According to Mr. Barber, obesity gave him diabetes, high blood pressure, and two heart attacks. When a reporter asked him why he ate there so often, he said, "I was single, it was quick, and I'm not a very good cook."

Barber's lawyer, Samuel Hirsch, says that the suit has two different purposes. The first is to make fast-food restaurants offer healthier foods in smaller amounts. The suit also asks that fast foods have warning labels similar to labels on cigarettes. Mr. Hirsch says that these labels are necessary because the effects of fast foods are similar to the effects of cigarettes, alcohol, and illegal drugs such as heroin.

Two others may soon join Barber's suit. One is Frances Winn, a 57-year-old retired nurse. Ms. Winn says that she has eaten at fast-food restaurants at least twice a week since 1975. She says that this habit has caused several health problems, including high blood pressure. Israel Bradley, 59, said eating a pound of french fries every week gave him high blood pressure and diabetes.

Officials of the fast-food industry attacked the legal action. National Restaurant Association representative Katharine Kim called it ridiculous. KFC spokeswoman Amy Sherwood claimed KFC offers several kinds of foods for people who want to eat healthier. Legal expert Walter Olson agreed that the suit had little chance of success. He said that people were free to make different choices.

Whether or not the suit is successful, there is no doubt that Americans have a weight problem. Medical experts say that obesity will soon be America's number one killer. They have encouraged fast-food companies to offer healthier foods.

Read Again

Read the text a second time. As you read,
- underline the main idea in each paragraph.
- try to figure out the meaning of important unknown terms.

Read for the third time and do the following:
- use connectors to follow ideas.
- pay more attention to parts that confuse you.

Post-Reading Activities

A. Comprehension Check

Answer these questions about the reading.

1. Why is Caesar Barber suing fast-food companies?
2. What does he want the fast-food companies to do?
3. According to Barber's lawyer, what are the effects of eating fast food?
4. What do the fast-food companies think about the suit?

B. Vocabulary Check

Work with a partner to answer these questions.

1. Find a compound word in the reading. Write it here, and explain its meaning.

   ____

2. Find a synonym for *legal action* in the reading. Write it here. ____________
3. Circle the word(s) below with a suffix meaning "a person who or that which."

   healthier   killer   pressure   reporter   similar

4. Complete the chart for these words from the reading.

Word or Phrase	Do I know this word or phrase?	Is it important?	Is there an internal definition?	Other Clues		
				Is it a noun? verb? adjective?	Does it look like a word I know?	Can I use world knowledge?
1. suing						
2. obesity						
3. diabetes						
4. illegal						
5. aim						
6. warning labels						
7. illegal						
8. attacked						
9. ridiculous						

What other words did you not know? If they are important to the main idea, list them here:

____

C. Following Ideas

Write the word or phrase each item refers to. If the item does not refer to any word or phrase, put an "X" in the chart.

Word	Line	Refers to
1. these restaurants	6	
2. this diet	7	
3. there	10	
4. this habit	25	
5. they	41	

D. Identifying the Main Idea

Write the main idea of each of the following paragraphs.

paragraph 2 _____

3 _____

4 _____

Remember

Use a graphic organizer to chart the argument in the reading. Have a classmate explain your diagram to you.

Discuss

1. Do you agree with Mr. Barber? Why or why not?
2. If Mr. Barber wins his lawsuit, how much money should he get? Support your opinion.

4. READING

Prepare

This reading contains two letters. Work with a partner to answer these questions based on both letters. Explain your answers to the class.

1. What is the topic? Look at titles and subtitles of the texts.
2. Look at the other features of the texts. Make predictions about the following items.
   - a. genre
   - b. audience
   - c. purpose
   - d. difficulty

3. Brainstorm *fast-food restaurants* and their effects on foreign countries. List words and phrases for good and bad effects.

4. What will the first letter say about hamburgers "taking over"? What will the second letter say? Think of one question to ask each text. Write them down.

Read

Read the two letters to get a general idea of the meaning. Don't try to figure out unfamiliar terms. As you read, think of the questions you wrote in number 3 of the *Prepare* section. Mark key words and sections as you read.

The Times

Letters to the Editor

Americans are taking over the world with hamburgers!
(reprint of May 1st edition letter)

Dear Editor:

1   People around the world may not know it, but our cultures are in danger. The danger does not come from guns or bullets. The danger looks innocent. It is American fast food. Look around. There are few countries in the world today that do not have American fast-food restaurants. Hamburger giant McDonald's has been especially successful.

2   The facts speak for themselves. In 1988, McDonald's had only 2,600 restaurants abroad. By 1994, they had over 4,500 restaurants in 73 other countries. Today, there are more than 8,000 McDonald's restaurants in 101 countries. The most popular restaurant in Japan is McDonald's, with Kentucky Fried Chicken in second place. Today, France has 760 McDonald's restaurants; Australia, 680; Germany, 743; United Kingdom and Canada, 1,200. When McDonald's opened its first restaurant in Minsk, over 4,000 Belorussians came to eat. The manager had to call the police to control the crowds. Today, the largest McDonald's restaurant overlooks Tiananmen Square in Beijing. There are now 127 McDonald's in China, and more are planned.

3   Think of all of the money that American corporations are making from other countries. McDonald's international business is already a very important part of its annual sales. In fact, 59 percent of its profits come from restaurants outside the United States. And this amount is likely to increase. Every day, three new McDonald's restaurants open someplace in the world.

4   Many of us are not pleased about the great success of American fast-food restaurants. Each country has its own kind of foods. These foods are disappearing, and our diets are being Americanized. In my opinion, American businesses like McDonald's are destroying our cultures. We have to stop them now!
—F. G.

Don't Blame the Americans

Dear Editor,

5   I don't agree with the editorial that appeared in your paper on May 1. The writer claimed that American fast-food restaurants are destroying cultures around the world. In my opinion, this is totally untrue.

6   There are many reasons for the success of fast-food chains like McDonald's. First of all, they have adapted to foreign tastes. For instance, McDonald's sells wine in France, black currant

milkshakes in Poland, salads with shrimp in Germany, vegetarian burgers in the Netherlands and India, tatsuta chicken sandwiches (with ginger and soy sauce) in Japan, and a salmon sandwich called McLaks in Norway. In addition, other factors contributing to fast-food success abroad are cleanliness, a family atmosphere, air conditioning, and efficient service.

7   It's ridiculous to say that American fast food is destroying other cultures. First, the owners of these franchises are usually not Americans. They are businesspeople from that country. Second, no one is making anyone buy hamburgers. If people refuse to eat fast food, then all the fast-food restaurants will close.

   Sincerely yours,
   James Morton

Read Again

Read the text a second time. As you read,

- think of another question and read to find the answer.
- underline the main idea of each letter.
- try to figure out the meaning of important unknown terms.

Read the text a third time. As you read,

- use connectors to follow ideas.
- use signal words to help you predict ideas.
- pay more attention to parts that confuse you.
- mark terms you could not figure out.

Post-Reading Activities

A. Comprehension Check

Mark each statement true (T), false (F), or cannot tell from the reading (X).

1. _____ McDonald's sells the McLaks sandwich in France.

2. _____ There are 4,000 McDonald's restaurants in Russia.

3. _____ The menu at McDonald's is not the same in every country.

4. _____ In some countries, people do not like fast food.

5. _____ Foods of other cultures are disappearing because of fast foods.

6. _____ KFC is more popular than McDonald's in Japan.

7. _____ Fast-food restaurants succeed because they are clean.

8. _____ No one is making anyone buy hamburgers.

9. _____ Turkey has more McDonald's restaurants than Brazil.

B. Vocabulary Check

Work with a partner to answer these questions.

1. List the foods mentioned in the reading. For each one, decide if you have to know exactly what these foods are, and why or why not.

   a. _____ _____

   b. _____ _____

   c. _____ _____

   d. _____ _____

   e. _____ _____

   f. _____ _____

2. Complete the chart for these words from the reading.

Word	Do I know this word?	Is it important?	Is there an internal definition?	Other Clues		
				Is it a noun? verb? adjective?	Does it look like a word I know?	Can I use world knowledge?
1. cultures						
2. giant						
3. abroad						
4. Belorussians						
5. overlooks						
6. Tiananmen						
7. adapted						
8. pleased						
9. Americanized						
10. cleanliness						
11. atmosphere						

What other words did you not know? If they are important to the main idea, list them here:

_____

C. Following Ideas

Write the word or phrase each item refers to. If the item does not refer to any word or phrase, put an "X" in the chart.

Words	Line	Refers to
1. our cultures	2	
2. they	11	
3. there	12	
4. its	28	
5. this amount	30	
6. one	63	

D. Predicting Ideas with Signal Words

Work with a partner. Use the signal words to unscramble the paragraph. Do not look at the reading. Rewrite the paragraph, putting the four sentences in the correct order.

For instance, McDonald's sells wine in France, black currant milk shakes in Poland, salads with shrimp in Germany, vegetarian burgers in the Netherlands and India, tatsuta chicken sandwiches (with ginger and soy sauce) in Japan, and a salmon sandwich called McLaks in Norway. First of all, they have adapted to foreign tastes. There are many reasons for the success of fast-food chains like McDonald's. In addition, other factors contributing to fast-food success abroad are cleanliness, a family atmosphere, air conditioning, and efficient service.

E. Identifying the Main Idea
Find the main idea of each of the following paragraphs.

paragraph 1 _____

2 _____

3 _____

4 _____

7 _____

Remember

Diagram the idea of paragraph 4. Show how fast-food restaurants destroy the foods of other cultures. Use a flowchart or other diagram.

Discuss

1. Are there many American fast-food restaurants in your country? Which ones?
2. What effect do you think these restaurants have on your culture?

Reviewing Your Reading

A. Look at the following list of readings in this chapter. Check the column that shows how easy or difficult the material was for you.

Name of Reading	Easy	Average	Difficult
1. The Growth of Fast Food in the United States			
2. Nutritional Chart for Adult Men and Women			
3. Man Sues Fast-Food Companies for Health Problems			
4. Letters to the Editor: (1) Americans are taking over the world with hamburgers!			
(2) Don't Blame the Americans			

B. Read the following list of strategies that you have practiced in this chapter. Review the readings. Check which strategies you used, and how often you used them.

Strategy	Always	Often	Sometimes	Never
Prepare				
Making predictions about the text: audience, genre, purpose, content, and difficulty				
Read/Read Again				
Identifying the main idea				
Using connectors (*this, that, these, those, there, one*) to follow ideas				
Using signal words to predict ideas				
Remember				
Using graphic organizers				
Vocabulary Strategies				
Using grammar				
Using word forms				
Using world knowledge				

Reading: Underground World

7

Getting Started

Discuss these questions in pairs or small groups. Share your ideas with the class.

1. What is the "underground world"?
2. Are there famous caves in your country? What are they?
3. Have you been in a cave? Describe the experience.

Strategies Reminder

Comprehension Strategies

Prepare
- Making Predictions about the Text

Read
- Identifying the Main Idea
- Using Connectors (*this, that, these, those, there, one*) to Follow Ideas
- More Practice Using Signal Words to Predict Ideas

Remember
- Using Graphic Organizers

Vocabulary Strategies
- Using Grammar
- Using Word Forms
- Using World Knowledge

1 READING

Prepare

Work with a partner to answer these questions. Explain your answers to the class.

1. What type of reading is this? What type of reader is it written for?
2. Will the text be difficult to read? Why or why not?
3. Exchange information about caves with another pair. Prepare a list of terms.
4. Ask the text a question. Write it down to remember it.

Read

Read the text to get a general idea of the meaning. Don't try to figure out unfamiliar terms. As you read, think of the question you wrote in number 4 of the *Prepare* section. Mark key words and sections as you read.

MODERN GEOLOGY

Volume 2: Caves

Some Cave Basics

Caves are fascinating places because no cave is exactly like another. Many caves have rivers, and some even have waterfalls. Some caves are only large enough for one person. Others are many miles long. Some caves are quite beautiful. They have multicolored walls and tall columns. Columns that come up from the floor are known as *stalagmites*. Columns that hang from the ceiling are called *stalactites*.

People have been interested in caves since prehistoric times. People in the Stone Age lived in caves. You can still see their paintings of animals on cave walls. Today, cave exploration is a sport. It is known as *spelunking*, or simply *caving*, in the United States, and *potholing* in Britain. The scientific study of caves is called *speleology*.

Formation of Caves

Most caves are found in limestone rock. Limestone dissolves in water. As water moves through cracks in the limestone, it dissolves the rock. In this way, the cracks get larger and larger. They eventually form large spaces. The water in a cave contains a lot of dissolved limestone. When this water evaporates into the air, the limestone is left. When water drops from the roof of a cave for thousands of years, stalactites and stalagmites form.

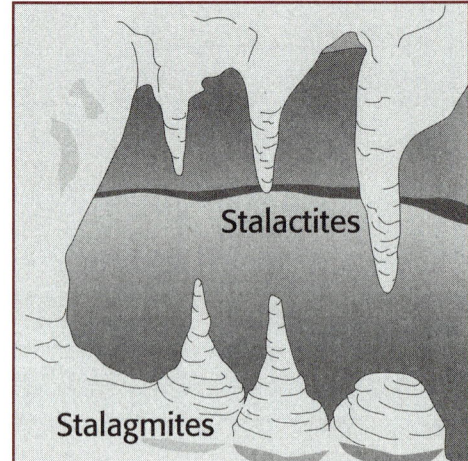

Special Kinds of Caves

A small number of caves are found in other kinds of rocks. For instance, in Hawaii and Iceland, there are caves in lava from volcanoes. Sometimes caves form in hard rocks such as granite. Granite caves are common along seashores. Water forms these caves too, but in a different way. The ocean waves gradually erode or wear away the rocks and leave large empty spaces. Some caves are not formed by water. For example, when gases from oil fields enter limestone, they carve out large caves. The Big Room of Carlsbad Caverns in New Mexico was formed in this way.

Read Again

Read the text a second time. As you read,

- think of two more questions and read to find the answers.
- underline the main ideas.
- try to figure out the meaning of important unknown terms.

Read the text a third time. As you read,

- use connectors to follow ideas.
- pay more attention to parts that confuse you.
- think of more strategies to figure out unknown terms.

Post-Reading Activities

A. Comprehension Check

Make true statements based on the reading. Complete the sentences with correct phrases from the list.

All caves   Most caves   Some caves   No caves

1. _____ are underground.

2. _____ are made of limestone.

3. _____ are found in granite and lava.

4. _____ are large.

5. _____ are formed by water.

6. _____ are formed by gas.

7. _____ have stalactites and stalagmites.

8. _____ are exactly alike.

9. _____ have waterfalls.

B. Vocabulary Check

Work with a partner to answer these questions.

1. List some types of rock mentioned in the reading. Do you have to know exactly what these rocks are? Why or why not?

   a. _____ b. _____ c. _____

2. Complete the chart for these words from the reading.

Word or Phrase	Do I know this word or phrase?	Is it important?	Is there an internal definition?	Is there an illustration?	Other Clues		
					Is it a noun? verb? adjective?	Does it look like a word I know?	Can I use world knowledge?
1. multicolored							
2. columns							
3. stalagmites							
4. stalactites							
5. prehistoric							
6. Stone Age							
7. spelunking							
8. potholing							
9. speleology							
10. cracks							

Word or Phrase	Do I know this word or phrase?	Is it important?	Is there an internal definition?	Is there an illustration?	Other Clues		
					Is it a noun? verb? adjective?	Does it look like a word I know?	Can I use world knowledge?
11. dissolves							
12. evaporates							
13. erode							

What other words did you not know? If they are important to the main idea, list them here:

_____

C. Following Ideas

Write the word or phrase each item refers to. If the item does not refer to any word or phrase, put an "X" in the chart.

Word or Phrase	Line	Refers to
1. it	8	
2. it	12	
3. this way	13	
4. this water	16	
5. they	24	
6. The Big Room	24	

Remember

Draw a process diagram to show how a cave forms in limestone rock.

Discuss

1. Name other things, besides limestone, that dissolve in water. Try to explain the basic process.
2. In addition to limestone, what erodes rock? What erodes soil?

3. _____ are found in granite and lava.

4. _____ are large.

5. _____ are formed by water.

6. _____ are formed by gas.

7. _____ have stalactites and stalagmites.

8. _____ are exactly alike.

9. _____ have waterfalls.

B. Vocabulary Check

Work with a partner to answer these questions.

1. List some types of rock mentioned in the reading. Do you have to know exactly what these rocks are? Why or why not?

   a. _____   b. _____   c. _____

2. Complete the chart for these words from the reading.

Word or Phrase	Do I know this word or phrase?	Is it important?	Is there an internal definition?	Is there an illustration?	Other Clues: Is it a noun? verb? adjective?	Other Clues: Does it look like a word I know?	Other Clues: Can I use world knowledge?
1. multicolored							
2. columns							
3. stalagmites							
4. stalactites							
5. prehistoric							
6. Stone Age							
7. spelunking							
8. potholing							
9. speleology							
10. cracks							

Word or Phrase	Do I know this word or phrase?	Is it important?	Is there an internal definition?	Is there an illustration?	Other Clues		
					Is it a noun? verb? adjective?	Does it look like a word I know?	Can I use world knowledge?
11. dissolves							
12. evaporates							
13. erode							

What other words did you not know? If they are important to the main idea, list them here:

_____

C. Following Ideas

Write the word or phrase each item refers to. If the item does not refer to any word or phrase, put an "X" in the chart.

Word or Phrase	Line	Refers to
1. it	8	
2. it	12	
3. this way	13	
4. this water	16	
5. they	24	
6. The Big Room	24	

Remember

Draw a process diagram to show how a cave forms in limestone rock.

Discuss

1. Name other things, besides limestone, that dissolve in water. Try to explain the basic process.
2. In addition to limestone, what erodes rock? What erodes soil?

2. READING

Prepare

Work with a partner to answer these questions. Explain your answers to the class.

1. Will this reading give mostly facts, opinions, or descriptions? How do you know?
2. What is the purpose of the text? Who will probably read it?
3. Brainstorm *caving* and *equipment*. What do you need to go caving?
4. What will you learn about caving? Write down two questions.

Read

Read the text to get a general idea of the meaning. Don't try to figure out unfamiliar terms. As you read, think of the questions you wrote in number 5 of the *Prepare* section. Mark key words and sections as you read.

Caving Equipment

Before you start caving, be sure you have the mandatory equipment.

Lights and Helmets

Caves are absolutely dark, so you must carry light with you. Two of the common types are electric lights and carbide lights.

Electric lights are a kind of flashlight. The light on the left in the picture (#1) is an example. This unit is called the "Zoom Headlight," by Hobb Electronics. It costs about $40 (U.S.).

The more traditional lighting unit is a carbide lamp (see #2 in the picture). A carbide lamp produces light by burning acetylene gas. Carbide lamps can be bought through The Outdoor Store. They cost about $50.

Rocks often fall in caves, so the other necessary item is a helmet to protect your head. You can buy a good helmet for about $25. There are a number of other items that are not necessary but can be useful for cave exploration.

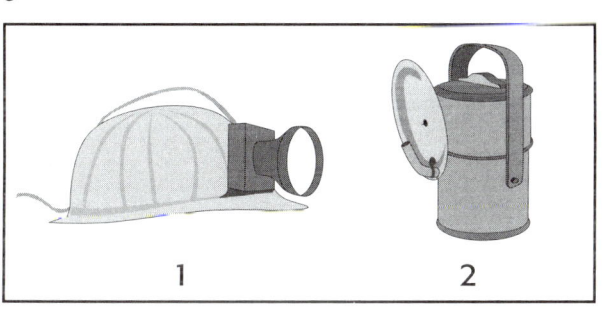

Clothing and Accessories

Caves destroy ordinary clothes. Therefore, it's good to wear coveralls. Pictured here is a flight suit made by Franconia that costs about $40.

Boots are another useful item. Good boots cost around $35. There are two kinds—army boots or jungle boots. Army boots are waterproof—no water can get in; jungle boots have holes around the bottom. Army boots will keep your feet dry, unless the water gets in at the top. If this happens, the water will stay in the boots. Your feet will get wet in jungle boots, but they will allow the water to drain. Both types of boots are available at The Outdoor Store.

Gloves are important to protect your hands. Leather and canvas gardening gloves work well and only cost about $4. You can buy these at any hardware store.

Kneepads are necessary in caves with low ceilings. They come in many styles. They can be found at hardware stores or sporting goods stores.

It's also good to have a small backpack to carry water bottles, chemical heaters for emergencies, an extra battery, and food. You can buy special ones for caving, or just get a hiking daypack at a sporting goods store.

Experience

That is about it for equipment to start caving, but you still need experience. Before you enter a cave, it is important that you have an experienced caver with you. Look for a caving club in your area. There you will be able to meet people who can help you get started.

Read Again

Read the text a second time. As you read,

- think of another question and read to find the answer.
- underline the reason why each piece of equipment is important.
- try to figure out the meaning of important unknown terms.

Read the text a third time. As you read,

- use connectors to follow ideas.
- use signal words to help you predict ideas.
- pay more attention to parts that confuse you.

Post-Reading Activities

A. Comprehension Check

Scan the reading for the following information. Write the answers in the blanks.

1. two kinds of lights cavers use   _____   _____

2. the kind of energy each light uses   _____   _____

3. cost of a helmet   _____

4. two kinds of boots cavers wear   _____   _____

5. why kneepads are important   _____

B. Vocabulary Check

Work with a partner to answer these questions.

1. Circle the words that are not clothing and accessories for caving.

   batteries ceilings coveralls heaters helmets kneepads

2. Complete the chart for these words from the reading.

Word or Phrase	Do I know this word or phrase?	Is it important?	Is there an internal definition?	Is there an illustration?	Other Clues		
					Is it a noun? verb? adjective?	Does it look like a word I know?	Can I use world knowledge?
1. mandatory							
2. absolutely							
3. caving							
4. equipment							
5. traditional							
6. acetylene gas							
7. ordinary							
8. army							
9. jungle							
10. waterproof							
11. drain							
12. gardening							
13. ceilings							

What other words did you not know? If they are important to the main idea, list them here:

____

C. Following Ideas

Write the word or phrase each item refers to. If the item does not refer to any word or phrase, put an "X" in the chart.

Word or Phrase	Line	Refers to
1. this unit	5	
2. there	15	
3. it's	18	
4. that	20	
5. this	26	
6. they	28	
7. that	42	
8. there	46	

D. Predicting Ideas with Signal Words

1. Scan the reading for signal words and circle them.
2. Compare your answers with a classmate's. Did you both find the same words? Explain your choices.

Remember

Complete this chart with information from the reading.

Caving Equipment	Purpose	Cost

Discuss

1. What are some other sports you enjoy? What equipment do you use?
2. Are some sports too expensive for most people to do? Why or why not?

3 READING

Prepare

Work with a partner to answer these questions. Explain your answers to the class.

1. What does the title mean? What will the reading be about?
2. Think about things that destroy caves. Prepare a list of terms you expect to see.
3. What will the reading say about saving the Big Room? Ask the text two questions.

Read

Read the text to get a general idea of the meaning. Don't try to figure out unfamiliar terms. As you read, think of the questions you wrote in number 3 of the *Prepare* section. Mark key words and phrases as you read.

To Save a Cave

In November 1974, two young cavers, Gary Tenen and Randy Tufts, were exploring the limestone hills in the Whetstone Mountains in Arizona. There they found a small hole in the hillside. Warm, moist air was coming out. The hole was too small to enter, so they started digging to enlarge it. After several hours, they were able to squeeze through, and they found themselves in a large cavern. When they turned on their powerful carbide lights, they realized that they were standing in a 300-foot-long cave. They named it the Big Room.

For a long time, Tenen and Tufts told only a few people about the cave. They waited four years to tell the property owners, James and Lois Kartchner. The young men had good reason to keep quiet: They knew that if people knew about the cave, they might destroy it.

"Our whole purpose since day one has been to protect the cave," says Mr. Tufts. "Historically, caves like this have been vandalized terribly by people who spray paint on walls, break the formations, leave trash. It doesn't take long to destroy a cave. We didn't want to see that happen, so we eventually decided the only way to protect it was to develop it."

The cave's existence was announced to the public in 1988, when the state of Arizona bought it to make a park and named it the Kartchner Cave after the property owners. State officials and speleologists have worked hard to protect the cave. This is because Kartchner is a "live" cave. Many of the rock formations have been growing for tens of thousands of years. They want to make certain that they will continue to grow.

Vandalism is not the only danger to a cave. Caves can be destroyed in a number of other ways. For example, the stalactites and stalagmites are extremely fragile, so visitors are not allowed to touch them. In addition, light isn't good for a cave. The heat from lights can dry it out, and light allows algae to grow. Algae can destroy the beautiful colors of the rocks. Therefore, computers control the lights in the Kartchner caves. Dry air from the outside can also destroy a cave. Even a small change in the humidity can stop stalagmites and stalactites from growing. In order to keep the humidity at 98 percent all the time, the Kartchner caves are protected by special doors.

Both Tenet and Tufts are hopeful that all these measures will help to keep the Kartchner Cave beautiful and growing for years to come.

120 CHAPTER 7

Read Again

Read the text a second time. As you read,

- think of more questions and read to find the answers.
- underline the main idea of each paragraph.
- try to figure out the meaning of important unknown terms.

Read the text a third time. As you read,

- use connectors to follow ideas.
- use signal words to help you predict ideas.
- pay more attention to parts that confuse you.

Post-Reading Activities

A. Comprehension Check

Answer these questions about the reading.

1. Why are these three dates important? 1974 1978 1988
2. Why did the two boys keep the cave a secret?
3. Who can visit the cave now?
4. What three things can hurt a cave? How can they hurt it?
5. Why isn't the Kartchner Cave called the "Tenen and Tufts Cave"?

B. Vocabulary Check

Work with a partner to answer these questions.

1. Find and circle a synonym for *cave* in the reading. Write it here. _____

   _____

2. Find two words related to *vandal*. What do they mean? _____

   _____

3. Complete the chart for these words from the reading.

Word	Do I know this word?	Is it important?	Is there an internal definition?	Is there an illustration?	Other Clues		
					Is it a noun? verb? adjective?	Does it look like a word I know?	Can I use world knowledge?
1. through							
2. moist							

Word	Do I know this word?	Is it important?	Is there an internal definition?	Is there an illustration?	Other Clues		
					Is it a noun? verb? adjective?	Does it look like a word I know?	Can I use world knowledge?
3. enlarge							
4. squeeze							
5. historically							
6. vandalized							
7. trash							
8. existence							
9. fragile							
10. algae							
11. humidity							

What other words did you not know? If they are important to the main idea, list them here:

_____

C. Following Ideas

Write the word or phrase each item refers to. If the item does not refer to any word or phrase, put an "X" in the chart.

Word or Phrase	Line	Refers to
1. there	3	
2. the young men	14–15	
3. this	20	
4. that	23	
5. this	29	
6. they	32	
7. it	39	
8. these measures	47–48	

D. Predicting Ideas with Signal Words

The following signal words are found in the reading. Predict the **type** of idea that came before each one. Check the text to see if your guesses are correct.

a. *after* _____

b. *for example* _____

c. *in addition* _____

d. *therefore* _____

E. Identifying the Main Idea

This reading can be divided into two parts. Write the main idea of each part. Then write a subtitle for each part.

Part 1 Main Idea _____

_____

Subtitle _____

Part 2 Main Idea _____

_____

Subtitle _____

Remember

Complete the following chart with key facts from the reading. The first problem is listed for you.

How Can You Keep a Cave Alive?	
Problem	**Solution**
1. vandalism	
2.	
3.	

Discuss

1. Should governments spend money to save a cave? Support your opinion.
2. What caves or other natural places in your country would you save? Why?

4. READING

Prepare

Work with a partner to answer these questions. Explain your answers to the class.

1. Look at the title of the reading and the photo. What is the topic?
2. Look at the other features. Make predictions.
3. Will the text answer this question: "How many people see the gardens every year?"

Read

Read the text to get a general idea of the meaning. Don't try to figure out unfamiliar terms. As you read, think of the question stated in number 3 of the *Prepare* section. Mark key words and sections as you read.

One Man's Dream
The History of the Forestiere Underground Gardens

1 In 1905, Baldasare Forestiere, an immigrant from Sicily, arrived in Fresno, California. There he bought a piece of land. He dreamed of growing trees and vines. Unfortunately, Baldasare discovered that his land was hardpan, or hard dirt, that is completely useless for agriculture.

However, Baldasare was unwilling to give up his dream, so he began to dig. Over the next 40 years, he carved out an underground wonderland of courtyards, patios, rooms, and passageways. In all, he made more than 50 rooms and 100 patios and courtyards—all beneath 10 acres of land. Amazingly, he used only hand tools, and when he died in 1946, he had spent a total of only $300 on supplies.

The Underground Gardens are an awesome sight. They are full of life and light. Skylights and courtyards let in sunlight and rainwater for the fruit trees and grapevines. The rock ceilings and walls protect them from the heat above and the frost below. Above the ground, where their tops emerge, the trees look like bushes.

The gardens also made an unusual home for Baldasare. There are beds built into the walls, a bathtub carved into the rock, and long tunnels that go from one end to another. All of this was the work of a dreamer who was unwilling to give up. As Baldasare said, "To make something with lots of money, that is easy—but to make something out of nothing . . . now that is something." Baldasare died in 1946 at the age of 67. After his death, the Underground Gardens were opened to the public as a museum.

The Underground Gardens are open from Wednesday through Sunday, 10 A.M. to 4 P.M. Tours run on the hour and are by advance reservation only.

Admission:
Adults $6.00
Seniors/students $5.00
Children 5+ $3.00
Children under 5 free

For more information and for reservations, please call.
Forestiere Underground Gardens
5021 W. Shaw Avenue
Fresno, CA 93722
(559) 555-0734

Read Again

Read the text a second time. As you read,

- think of three more questions and read to find the answers.
- note that the reading has two different parts. Decide the topic of each part.
- try to figure out the meaning of important unknown terms.

Read the text a third time. As you read,

- use connectors to follow ideas.
- use signal words to help you predict ideas.
- pay more attention to parts that confuse you.
- think of more strategies to figure out unknown words.

Post-Reading Activities

A. Comprehension Check

Answer these questions about the reading.

1. Who built the Underground Gardens and why?
2. Where are the Underground Gardens?
3. How did Baldasare build them?
4. How many rooms do the gardens have?
5. What kinds of plants are in the Underground Gardens?
6. Did Baldasare live underground?
7. How much does it cost to visit the museum?
8. How can you contact the museum?

B. Vocabulary Check

Work with a partner. Complete the chart for these words from the reading.

Word or Phrase	Do I know this word or phrase?	Is it important?	Is there an internal definition?	Is there an illustration?	Other Clues		
					Is it a noun? verb? adjective?	Does it look like a word I know?	Can I use world knowledge?
1. hardpan							
2. agriculture							
3. unwilling							
4. carved out							
5. wonderland							
6. courtyards							
7. patios							
8. beneath							
9. acres							
10. skylights							
11. frost							
12. emerge							
13. tunnels							

What other words did you not know? If they are important to the main idea, list them here:

_____

C. Following Ideas

Write the word or phrase each item refers to. If the item does not refer to any word or phrase, put an "X" in the chart.

Word	Line	Refers to
1. there	2	
2. them	20	
3. all of this	26	
4. that	29	
5. that	30	

Remember

List key facts from the reading. Then draw a cluster diagram to organize the information.

What? _____

Where? _____

When? _____

Why? _____

How? _____

Who? _____

Discuss

1. Reread the quote from Forestiere. Do you agree with him? Why or why not?
2. Was Forestiere's project worthwhile? Why or why not?

Reviewing Your Reading

A. Look at the following list of readings in this chapter. Check the column that shows how easy or difficult the material was for you.

Name of Reading	Easy	Average	Difficult
1. Modern Geology: Some Cave Basics			
2. Caving Equipment			
3. To Save a Cave			
4. One Man's Dream			

B. Read the following list of strategies that you have practiced in this chapter. Review the readings. Check which strategies you used, and how often you used them.

Strategy	Always	Often	Sometimes	Never
Prepare				
Making predictions about the text: audience, genre, purpose, content, and difficulty				
Read/Read Again				
Identifying the main idea				
Using connectors (*this, that, these, those, there, one*) to follow ideas				
Using signal words to predict ideas				
Remember				
Using graphic organizers				
Vocabulary Strategies				
Using grammar				
Using word forms				
Using world knowledge				

Reading: Numbers, Numbers, Numbers

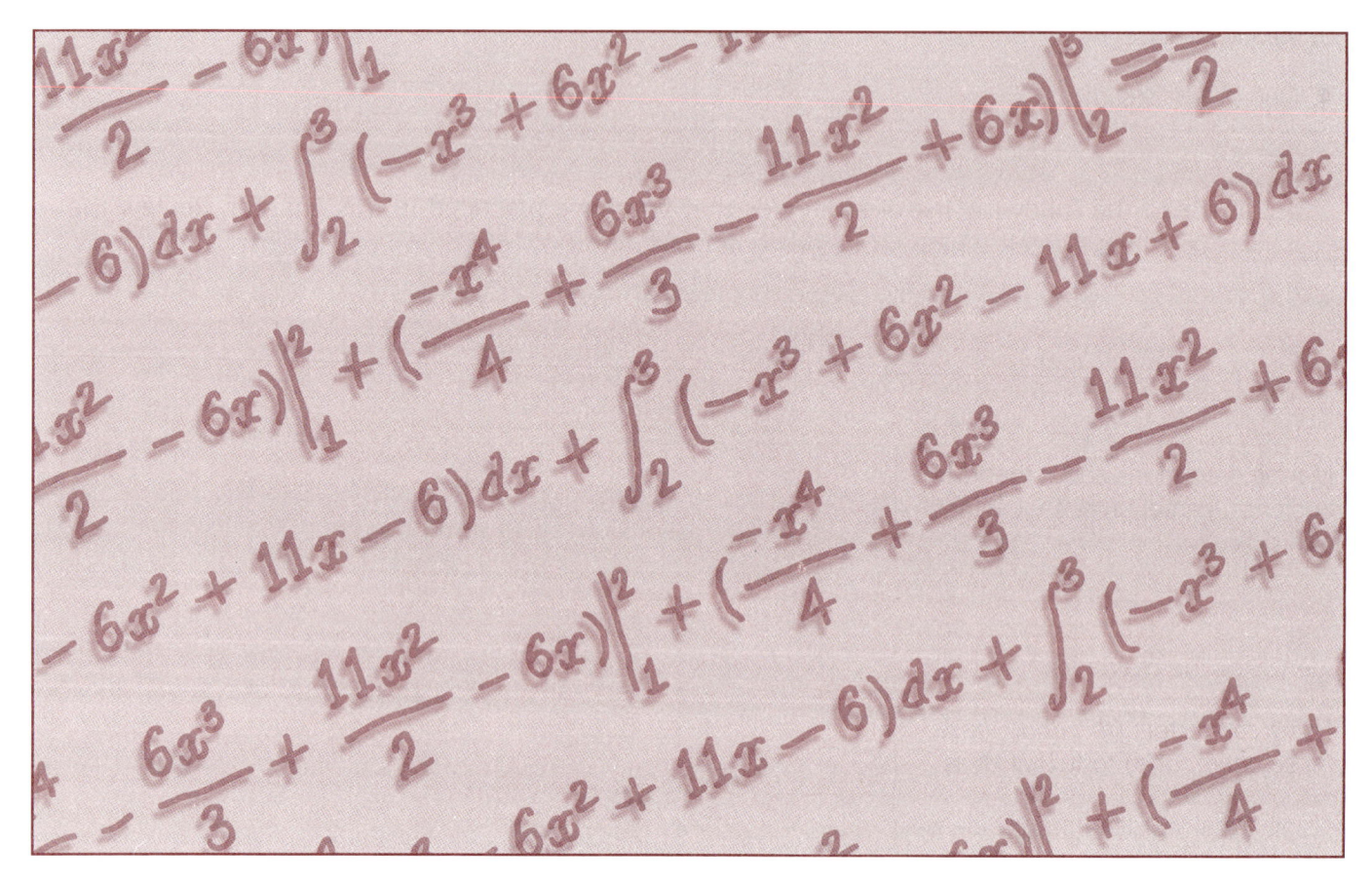

8

Getting Started

Discuss these questions in pairs or small groups. Share your ideas with the class.

1. Are you interested in mathematics? Why or why not?
2. Name four ways people figure numbers and amounts.
3. Look at the titles of the readings and the illustrations. What will this chapter say about numbers?

Strategies Reminder

Comprehension Strategies

Prepare
- Making Predictions about the Text

Read
- Identifying the Main Idea
- Using Connectors (*this, that, these, those, there, one*) to Follow Ideas
- More Practice Using Signal Words to Predict Ideas

Remember
- Using Graphic Organizers

Vocabulary Strategies
- Using Grammar
- Using Word Forms
- Using World Knowledge

1. READING

Prepare

Work with a partner to answer these questions. Explain your answers to the class.

1. Read the title of the reading. What is the meaning of *sense*?
2. Make predictions about the genre, audience, purpose, and difficulty of the reading.
3. Think about animals' sense of numbers. Have you ever seen a bird count eggs?
4. Think of a wh- question that you think the text might answer.

Read

Read the text to get a general idea of the meaning. Don't try to figure out unfamiliar terms. As you read, think of the question you wrote in number 4 of the *Prepare* section. Mark key words and sections as you read.

Making Sense of Numbers

1   Number sense is not the ability to count. It is the ability to recognize a change in number. Human beings are born with this ability. Surprisingly, experiments show that many animals are, too.

For instance, many birds have good number sense. If a nest has four eggs and you remove one, the bird will not notice. However, if you remove two, the bird generally leaves. This means that the bird knows the
5   difference between two and three.

Another interesting experiment demonstrated a bird's incredible number sense. A man was trying to photograph a crow that had a nest in a tower, but the crow always left when she saw him coming. The bird did not return until the man left the tower. The man had an idea. He took another man with him to the tower. One man left and the other stayed, but they didn't fool the crow. The crow stayed away until the second man left, too. The experiment was repeated with three men and then with four men. But the crow did not return to the nest until all the men were gone. It was not until five men went into the tower and only four left that they were able to fool the crow.

In the insect world, wasps seem to have the best number sense. The female wasp lays her eggs in individual cells and leaves caterpillars in each cell for the baby wasps to eat. Different kinds of wasps leave different numbers of caterpillars—some 5, others 12, and still others as many as 24 caterpillars per cell. One kind of wasp puts 5 caterpillars in the cell of a male (the male is smaller) and 10 caterpillars in the cell of a female.

How good is a human's number sense? It's not very good. For example, babies about 14 months old will almost always notice if something is taken away from a small group. But when the number goes beyond three or four, the children are often fooled. It seems that number sense is something that we share with many animals in this world, although our human ability is not much better than a crow's.

Read Again

Read the text a second time. As you read,

- think of a wh- question and read to find the answer.
- note the examples and points they illustrate.
- try to figure out the meaning of important unknown terms.

Read the text a third time. As you read,

- use connectors to follow ideas.
- use signal words to help you predict ideas.
- underline the main idea that each example illustrates.
- pay more attention to parts that confuse you.

Post-Reading Activities

A. Comprehension Check

Mark each statement true (T) or false (F).

1. _____ Number sense is the ability to count.

2. _____ Humans can count when they are born.

3. _____ The crow couldn't tell the difference between four and five.

4. _____ Wasps don't have very good number sense.

5. _____ Humans have excellent number sense by the time they are 14 months old.

6. _____ Human beings have about the same number sense as a wasp.

Numbers, Numbers, Numbers   **131**

B. Vocabulary Check

Work with a partner. Complete the chart for these words from the reading.

Word or Phrase	Do I know this word or phrase?	Is it important?	Is there an internal definition?	Other Clues: Is it a noun? verb? adjective?	Does it look like a word I know?	Can I use world knowledge?
1. number sense						
2. recognize						
3. notice						
4. incredible						
5. crow						
6. tower						
7. fool						
8. wasps						
9. lays						
10. cells						
11. caterpillars						

What other words did you not know? If they are important to the main idea, list them here:

_____

C. Following Ideas

Write the word or phrase each item refers to. If the item does not refer to any word or phrase, put an "X" in the chart.

Word or Phrase	Line	Refers to
1. this ability	2	
2. this	4	
3. she	7	
4. the other	9	

132   CHAPTER 8

Word or Phrase	Line	Refers to
5. it	11	
6. her	13	
7. the children	20	

D. Predicting Ideas with Signal Words

Use the signal words to unscramble the paragraph. Do not look at the reading. Rewrite the paragraph, putting the four sentences in the correct order.

This means that the bird knows the difference between two and three. However, if you remove two, the bird generally leaves. For instance, many birds have good number sense. If a nest has four eggs and you remove one, the bird will not notice.

_____

_____

_____

_____

_____

E. Identifying the Main Idea

Following are four examples of an animal's number sense. Each example proves a point. Name each point. Share your answers with the class.

1. eggs in the nest   _____

2. the crow   _____

3. the wasps   _____

4. 14-month old children   _____

Remember

Use a graphic organizer to chart the idea of paragraph 4.

Discuss

1. What are some other ways that number sense helps animals?
2. Are animals more intelligent than humans? Explain your answer.

2. READING

Prepare

Work with a partner to answer these questions. Explain your answers to the class.

1. How many parts does the reading have? What is the topic?
2. Make predictions. Predict audience, purpose, and difficulty.
3. Brainstorm the abacus. Name some terms you expect to see in each part of the text.
4. What will the text say about the abacus? Ask the text a question. Write it down.

Read

Read the text to get a general idea of the meaning. Don't try to figure out unfamiliar terms. As you read, think of the question you wrote in number 4 of the *Prepare* section. Mark key words and sections as you read.

The Abacus

What is an abacus?

An abacus is a manual calculator that is common in China, Korea, and Japan.

What does an abacus look like?

The frame of the abacus has several vertical rods. Each rod has a number of wooden beads that can move up and down. A horizontal piece separates the frame into two sections. These are known as the *upper deck* and the *lower deck*. The beads in the upper deck each have a value of 5. The beads on the lower deck each have a value of 1.

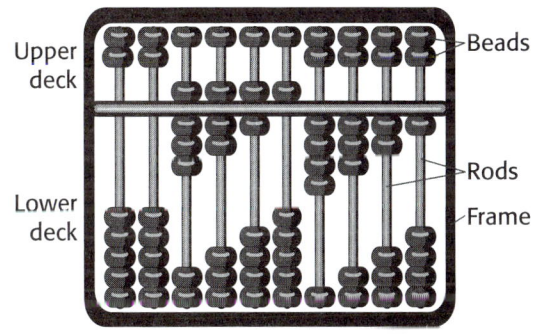

How are numbers counted?

Beads are counted by moving them toward the horizontal piece that separates the two decks. The rod on the far right is the ones column. The next is the tens column. The next is the hundreds column, and so on.

In the picture, the third column from the left represents the number 8. It has one bead from the top deck (value 5) and three beads from the bottom deck (each with a value of 1, totaling 3). The sum of the column (5 + 3) is 8.

Similarly, the fourth column represents the number 7. It has one bead from the top deck (value 5) and two beads from the bottom deck (each with a value of 1, totaling 2). The sum of the column (5 + 2) is 7.

Different types of abacuses

The Chinese abacus has two beads on the upper deck and five on the lower deck. This type of abacus is called a 2/5 abacus. The most popular Japanese abacus is a little different. It is called the 1/4 abacus because it has one bead on the top deck and four on the bottom.

Although the abacus is usually associated with Asia, people in other places in the world have developed them too. For example, archaeologists found a 1,000-year-old Aztec abacus in Mexico.

Read Again

Read the text a second time. As you read,

- think of more questions and read to find the answers.
- compare the text to the illustrations.
- underline main ideas.
- try to figure out the meaning of important unknown terms.

Read the text a third time. As you read,

- use connectors to follow ideas.
- use signal words to help you predict ideas.
- pay more attention to parts that confuse you.

Post-Reading Activities

A. Comprehension Check

Mark each statement true (T) or false (F).

1. _____ People in China and Japan do not uses abacuses today.

2. _____ The rods in an abacus are horizontal.

3. _____ Beads on an abacus move up and down.

4. _____ Every bead on an abacus has the same value.

5. _____ The beads on the upper deck have more value than the beads in the lower deck.

6. _____ The most popular abacus in Japan is the 2/5.

B. Vocabulary Check

Work with a partner. Complete the chart for these words from the reading.

Word	Do I know this word?	Is it important?	Is there an internal definition?	Is there an illustration?	Other Clues		
					Is it a noun? verb? adjective?	Does it look like a word I know?	Can I use world knowledge?
1. abacus							
2. manual							
3. calculator							

Numbers, Numbers, Numbers **135**

Word	Do I know this word?	Is it important?	Is there an internal definition?	Is there an illustration?	Other Clues		
					Is it a noun? verb? adjective?	Does it look like a word I know?	Can I use world knowledge?
4. frame							
5. vertical							
6. rod							
7. horizontal							
8. upper							
9. vertical							
10. deck							
11. bead							
12. value							
13. represents							
14. archaeologist							

C. Identifying the Main Idea

Write the main idea of each section in this reading.

1. What is an abacus? _____

2. What does an abacus look like? _____

3. How are numbers counted? _____

4. Different types of abacuses are _____.

Remember

Draw an abacus from memory. Show the number 57. Label each part.

Discuss

1. Have you ever used an abacus? Was it easy or difficult?
2. Some banks and other businesses continue to use the abacus. Is this a good idea? Why or why not?

3 · READING

Prepare

Work with a partner to answer these questions. Explain your answers to the class.

1. What is the topic of the reading? Predict from the title only.
2. This article came from a textbook. What was the subject of the textbook?
3. Brainstorm Roman numerals. List numerals you know and words connected to the topic.
4. What will you learn about "nothing"? Write your question down.

Read

Read the text to get a general idea of the meaning. Don't try to figure out unfamiliar terms. As you read, think of the question you wrote in number 4 of the *Prepare* section. Mark key words and sections as you read.

The Importance of Nothing

1 We think of the Romans as having a great empire. However, in one area the Romans were deficient. They never developed a number system that they could easily use for calculating. The system of Roman numerals was good for counting and recording amounts. However, even simple addition was a slow process.

2 To understand why, we have to examine the Roman number system. This system has seven symbols.

I = 1 (one)
V = 5 (five)
X = 10 (ten)
L = 50 (fifty)
C = 100 (one hundred)
D = 500 (five hundred)
M = 1000 (one thousand)

3 You can see that the Romans used one symbol for 5 (V), another for 50 (L), and still another for 500 (D). In order to represent some numbers, they had to repeat symbols. For instance, 3 was III, and 20 was XX. To represent other numbers, they had to add and subtract symbols. Therefore, IV (1, 5) represented 4, and VI (5, 1) represented 6.

4 The Arabic number system we use today is much simpler. It is made up of nine symbols, plus zero (0). Because of the zero (0), we can use the same symbol again and again. For example, 5 with one 0 is 50. With two 0s, it is 500.

5 With zero, a number system can use *position* to show amount. In our number system, the first column to the right of a whole number represents ones, the next is tens, the next is thousands, and so on.

thousands	hundreds	tens	ones
9	3	0	2

You use zero to hold a place when there is nothing in a column.

6   Using position makes the number system easier to understand in another important way: Longer numbers are bigger than shorter numbers. For example, 1,000 has four digits. It is longer than 999, which has only three. This is not true in Roman numerals. The number DCCCLXXXVIII (888) is much longer than M (1,000).

7   And look what happens when you try to multiply with Roman numerals. Every child today learns the multiplication tables in school.

    2 × 4 = 8   4 × 5 = 20   6 × 30 = 180

Children in Rome had to learn a much more complicated system.

    II × IV = VIII   IX × X = XC   VI × XXX = CLXXX

8   If the Romans didn't invent zero, who did? The zero was actually invented in India. The Indians developed a symbol for nothing (zero). This allowed them to create a system that made calculation easy.

Read Again

Read the text a second time. As you read,

- think of more questions and read to find the answers.
- note the examples and underline the points they illustrate.
- try to figure out the meaning of important unknown terms.

Read the text a third time. As you read,

- use connectors to follow ideas.
- use signal words to help you predict ideas.
- pay more attention to parts that confuse you.
- think of more strategies to figure out unknown terms.

Post-Reading Activities

A. Comprehension Check

Put an "X" in the correct column for each item.

	The Roman Number System	**The Arabic Number System**
1. has seven symbols		
2. has a zero		
3. is good for counting and recording amounts		
4. is easy to use for calculations		
5. uses position to show amounts		
6. has nine symbols		

B. Vocabulary Check

Work with a partner. Complete the chart for these words from the reading.

Word	Do I know this word?	Is it important?	Is there an internal definition?	Other Clues			
				Is it a noun? verb? adjective?	Does it look like a word I know?	Can I use world knowledge?	
1. deficient							
2. calculating							
3. addition							
4. symbol							
5. position							
6. digit							

What other words did you not know? If they are important to the main idea, list them here:

_____

C. Following Ideas

Write the word or phrase each item refers to. If the item does not refer to any word or phrase, put an "X" in the chart.

Word	Line	Refers to
1. they	1	
2. it	17	
3. there	24	
4. it	26	
5. this	35	

D. Predicting Ideas with Signal Words

Work with a partner to answer these questions. Share your answers with the class.

1. Scan the reading for these signal words and circle them.
    a. *because*
    b. *for instance*
    c. *however*
    d. *therefore*

2. List a similar term for each signal word listed in number 1.

   a. *because* _____

   b. *for instance* _____

   c. *however* _____

   d. *therefore* _____

3. Find the ideas the signal words connect. Restate them using the synonyms.

   a. *because* _____

   b. *for instance* _____

   c. *however* _____

   d. *therefore* _____

Remember

Use a graphic organizer to chart the disadvantages of the Roman number system.

Discuss

1. What are some ways Roman numerals are still used?
2. What were the number systems of other ancient peoples? If you lived in the Stone Age, did you use a number system?

4. READING

Prepare

Work with a partner to answer these questions. Explain your answers to the class.

1. What is the topic of the reading?
   a. an ancient people's numbers and calendar
   b. an ancient people's number system
   c. the ten-digit number system

2. Key terms connected to this topic will include:
   a. numbers, times, and digits.
   b. numbers, bars, and dots.
   c. Roman symbols.

3. The most important question this reading will answer is:
   a. Why did the Maya create a number system?
   b. Who were the Maya?
   c. What was the number system of the Maya?

Read

Read the text to get a general idea of the meaning. Don't try to figure out unfamiliar terms. As you read, think of the question you chose for number 3 from the *Prepare* section. Mark key words and sections as you read.

Mayan Numerals

1 The Maya had an excellent number system. In fact, they used a zero (0) hundreds of years before the Indians began using it. The Mayan number system was different from our Arabic number system in one important way: Instead of 10 digits like we have today, the Maya used a base number of 20. They used a system of bars and dots as shorthand for counting. A dot represented 1 and a bar represented 5.

2 In the illustration, you can see how the system of dots and bars works to create Mayan numerals.

3 Because the base of the number system was 20, larger numbers were written down in powers of 20. We do that in our decimal system too. For example, 32 is $3 \times 10 + 2$. In the Mayan system, this would be $1 \times 20 + 12$, because they used 20 as base.

4 The Maya used position to show amount just as we do. But instead of going from left to right, their numbers were written from bottom to top.

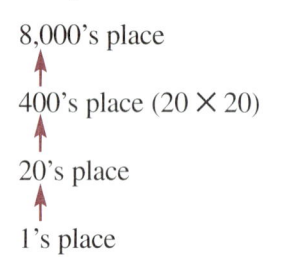

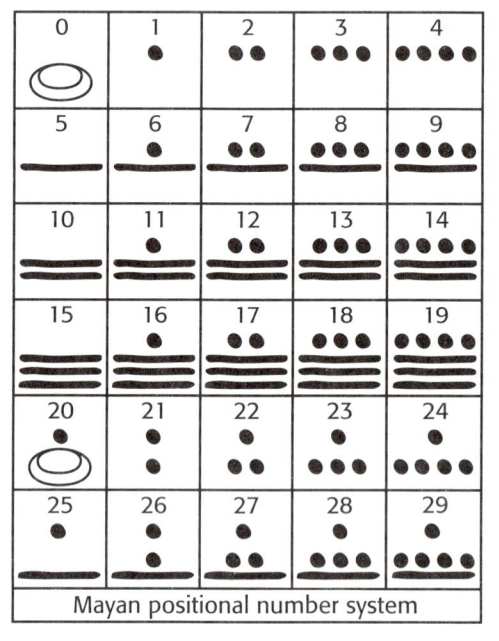

8,000's place
↑
400's place (20 × 20)
↑
20's place
↑
1's place

Below, you can see how the number 32 was written:

20's (1)
1's   (12)

5 It was easy to add and subtract using this number system. Here's an example of a simple addition:

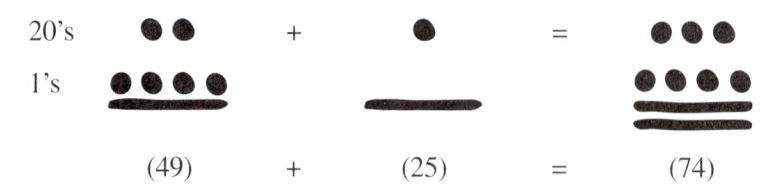

20's ●● + ● = ●●●
1's

(49) + (25) = (74)

30 **6** As you can see, adding is easy. You just have to count up the bars and dots. Mayan merchants often used cocoa beans, which they laid out on the ground, to do these calculations.

Read Again

Read the text a second time. As you read,

- think of wh- questions and read to find the answers.
- note the examples and underline the points they illustrate.
- try to figure out the meaning of important unknown terms.

Read the text a third time. As you read,

- use signal words to help you predict ideas.
- pay more attention to parts that confuse you.

Post-Reading Activities

A. Comprehension Check

Put an "X" in the correct column for each item.

	The Mayan Number System	The Arabic Number System
1. has two symbols		
2. has a zero (0)		
3. is easy to use for counting		
4. is easy to use for calculations		
5. uses position to show amounts		
6. writes numbers from bottom to top		

B. Vocabulary Check

Work with a partner to answer these questions.

1. What does *shorthand* mean? What kind of word is it? _____

_____

2. Find and circle a noun form of the verb *calculate*. What is its suffix? _____

_____

142   CHAPTER 8

3. Complete the chart for these words from the reading.

| Word or Phrase | Do I know this word or phrase? | Is it important? | Is there an internal definition? | Other Clues |||
				Is it a noun? verb? adjective?	Does it look like a word I know?	Can I use world knowledge?
1. base						
2. shorthand						
3. powers						
4. decimal						
5. cocoa beans						

What other words did you not know? If they are important to the main idea, list them here:

_____

C. Predicting Ideas with Signal Words

1. Scan the reading for signal words that are used in the following ways.

    a. contrast _____

    b. reason or cause _____

    c. example _____

2. Compare your list with a classmate's. Were your lists the same? If not, why not?

D. Identifying the Main Idea

Underline the main idea of the reading. What comparison helps make this idea clear?

Remember

Use picture notes to figure this equation by the Mayan system:

5,800 + 203 = 6,003

Discuss

1. The Maya counted by 20's; we count by 10's. Is counting by 5's a good idea? Why or why not?
2. Is the Mayan system easy to use? Explain your opinion.

Numbers, Numbers, Numbers **143**

Reviewing Your Reading

A. Look at the following list of the readings in this chapter. Check the column that shows how easy or difficult the material was for you.

Name of Reading	Easy	Average	Difficult
1. Making Sense of Numbers			
2. The Abacus			
3. The Importance of Nothing			
4. Mayan Numerals			

B. Read the following list of strategies that you have practiced in this chapter. Review the readings. Check which strategies you used, and how often you used them.

Strategy	Always	Often	Sometimes	Never
Prepare				
Making predictions about the text: audience, genre, purpose, content, and difficulty				
Read/Read Again				
Identifying the main idea				
Using connectors (*this, that, these, those, there, one*) to follow ideas				
Using signal words to predict ideas				
Remember				
Using graphic organizers				
Vocabulary Strategies				
Using grammar				
Using word forms				
Using world knowledge				

Reading Skills and Strategies

Overview of the Strategies

PART 1

Comprehension Strategies

Prepare
- Predicting from First and Last Paragraphs

Read
- Understanding Supporting Details
- Using Connectors (Ellipses) to Follow Ideas
- More Practice Using Signal Words to Predict Ideas
- Making Inferences
- Reading Difficult Material

Remember
- Outlining

PART 2

Vocabulary Strategies
- Using Grouping and Classification
- Using a Dictionary
- Understanding Abbreviations

PART 1 COMPREHENSION STRATEGIES

Prepare

Predicting from First and Last Paragraphs

There is a fast way to find a reading's main idea. Look at the beginning and the ending. Usually, the main idea is stated in one or both places.

Understanding the Strategy

The first paragraph usually introduces the main idea. The last paragraph often restates it or sums up key points. In articles and long texts, the main idea is given in a **thesis statement**. Skim beginnings and endings to search for the thesis statement.

Skim the first and last paragraphs to find the main idea of an article.

Example

First Paragraph

More and more Americans are starting home businesses. Among all the different kinds of home businesses, writing is probably the easiest. First of all, it is inexpensive. All you need is a typewriter, paper, stamps, an envelope, and a good public library. And, you may not believe it, but it isn't difficult to get started writing. That's because there are many kinds of writers. People write "how-to" books, computer manuals, company reports, cookbooks, dictionaries, and hundreds of other kinds of materials. Let's look at how you might begin your writing career from home.

Last Paragraph

These instructions for starting a writing business at home have worked for me and thousands of others. They can work for you, too. All you need is a dream and some confidence that you can make that dream come true.

Predictions

Topic: _writing at home as a business_

Main idea: _how to start a writing career at home_

ACTIVITY 1

Each item gives the beginning and ending of an article. Predict the topic and main idea. Compare your answers with classmates'. Explain your choices.

1.

First Paragraph

In the summer of 1995, my best friend Jack and I took a trip that changed our lives. Our trip took us to a foreign world, a place that we had never been. However, we didn't learn a new language or experience a different culture. We didn't even leave our own country. What did we do that changed our lives? We two city boys spent three months in the mountains, walking the Appalachian Trail from Georgia to Maine.

Last Paragraph

Jack and I are in the city again. We no longer spend our nights camped out under the stars. We don't have to worry about the weather anymore. And the only wild animals we see are the birds in the parks. But we will never forget our three-month adventure on the Appalachian Trail. We learned a lot about nature and gained confidence that we never had before.

Topic: _____

Main idea: _____

146 CHAPTER 9

2.

First Paragraph

Most parents think that they and their children are getting enough exercise. However, most of them are not, according to many doctors. And the results of a new study published by Farmington University Hospital seem to say that the doctors are right. So what should parents do?

Last Paragraph

It is possible to raise healthy children in today's world of television and fast food. However, parents must be realistic. They must understand how much exercise their children are really getting.

Topic: _____

Main idea: _____

Read

Understanding Supporting Details

Supporting details make ideas understandable. They try to prove a point. They should answer questions posed by the main idea, such as "Why?"; "What do you mean?"; or "Can you prove it?" Understanding details means both **identifying them** and **evaluating them**.

Understanding the Strategy

Supporting details describe, illustrate, or explain a point. Study the following types of supporting details to help you identify them in texts. Many types may be used to support the same point.

Identify supporting details as you read.

Types of Supporting Detail

The main idea is the first sentence in each of the following passages. The different types of supporting details follow the main idea. Note that some types of details are similar to others.

1 — Description

My granddaughter is a beautiful child. She has short curly black hair, big blue eyes, and rosy cheeks.

2 — Example

a. Our fire department doesn't protect us well. Recently, two people died in a fire because the firemen didn't arrive on time. A neighbor called the fire department soon after the fire started, but the fire trucks arrived 20 minutes later.

b. Never count your chickens before they hatch. That old saying is true! I didn't study for my test. I didn't think I needed to. I failed, and now I have to take the course again!

3 — Statistics

Teachers need higher salaries. The average salary has increased by 20 percent in the past six years. However, teachers' salaries are only 8 percent higher than they were six years ago.

4 — Experts

Christopher Columbus didn't discover America. According to the historian James Burke, civilizations existed in America before Columbus arrived.

5 — (Written) Facts

Thomas Jefferson was very creative. He made several inventions, including the first copy machine.

Example of identifying details:

The elderly need a doctor to supervise their medicine. One study showed that 20 percent of older adults are taking medicines that are not good for them. About 33 percent are taking unnecessary medicines. In fact, my elderly uncle William had to go to the hospital for taking pills he didn't need.

Main Idea: *The elderly need to have a doctor supervise their medicines.*

Type of Supporting Details: *statistics, example*

ACTIVITY 2 Read the paragraph. Underline the main idea. Identify the supporting details and their types.

Everyone knew that a job interview with Admiral Rickover was always difficult. Chances of success were slim; only one out of 100 men ever got hired. And anything might happen. At one time Rickover had a special chair for the men he interviewed. Its front legs were shorter than its back legs. While the interviewee tried to stay in the chair, the admiral asked him many difficult questions. In this way, the admiral tried to find smart men who could think quickly in difficult situations. These were the people he hired to work for him in the Navy.

Main Idea: _____

Supporting Details: _____

Type of Supporting Details: _____

Understanding the Strategy

Supporting details may provide weak, strong, or no support. They may or may not prove a point. At times, poor choices for details even prove the opposite point.

Evaluate details as you read.

Example of evaluating details:

Teachers should not give students homework on the weekends. First, <u>most students like to take a break then</u> and, in addition, <u>libraries are open on the weekend</u>.

Main Idea: *Teachers shouldn't give students homework on the weekends.*

Detail 1: *Weak. Being a student is a job, and a student's job is to study.*

Detail 2: *Supports the opposite point. (Student should have homework on the weekends so they can use the library.)*

ACTIVITY 3 Work as a class. Circle the letter of the details that support the main idea. Discuss why other choices are incorrect.

1. Humans are different from animals because they have language.
    a. Chimpanzees can learn languages.
    b. Dogs cannot speak.
    c. Every human community has a language.
    d. Spanish is easier to learn than Chinese.

2. Florida is a great place for a winter vacation.
    a. It has warm weather in December.
    b. It's a state.
    c. There are beautiful beaches.
    d. No one goes there in the summer.

3. Football should be the national sport of the United States.
    a. It's more exciting than baseball.
    b. More people attend football games than any other sport.
    c. There are more than 20 players on a team.
    d. The players make a lot of money.

Using Connectors to Follow Ideas

Using an ellipsis is another important way ideas are connected. An ellipsis is the short way to say something long. It is leaving words out to bring ideas closer together.

Understanding the Strategy

An ellipsis stresses the connection with what came before. It often occurs after signal words.

Learn to identify and understand ellipses.

after *and*
- this knife and [this] fork
- delicious fruits and [delicious] vegetables
- The boys [are ready] and girls are ready.
- We arrived on Tuesday and [we] left on Wednesday.

after *but*
- Johnny is smart but [he is] shy.
- I wanted to go, but he didn't [want to go].
- You can call him at night but [you cannot call] never in the morning.

after *or*
- Do you want coffee or [do you want] tea?
- Does he play the piano or [does he play] the guitar?
- Sam is going to buy an inexpensive sweater or [an inexpensive] shirt for Dan.

ACTIVITY 4   Look at the ellipses in the sentences. Then fill in the omitted, or missing, words.

1. My brother is fun-loving but _____ responsible.

2. Meryl is going to be a doctor or _____ a nurse.

3. I gave you that money to pay your rent and _____ your bills.

ACTIVITY 5   The symbol ▲ indicates an ellipsis. Draw an arrow to connect the ellipsis to the word or phrase it refers to.

1. The baby horse's legs were long and ▲ thin. They weren't strong now, but they would be ▲ soon.

2. For good luck, he carried a horseshoe and ▲ a rabbit's foot.

3. Fish is good for you, but beef isn't ▲.

4. He's going to London, ▲ not to Paris.

5. American cowboys wore boots, ▲ rode horses, and ▲ ate by a campfire.

6. Margaret asked her daughter to wash ▲ and put away the dishes.

Using Signal Words to Predict Ideas

Signal words serve many purposes in a text. Study the following new types, the examples, and the sample sentences.

More types and examples of signal words	
Contrast	*despite, in spite of, until*
Balancing contrasting points	*while*
Emphasizing similar points	*in fact*
Making clear	*in other words**
Time	*by + time, during, until, at that point/ time*

Sample Sentences

By 1999, Jenny was living in New York.
Despite her success, she was never happy.
When I visited her, she talked **during** movies.
She never stopped **until** we left the theater.
In spite of her bad behavior, I felt sorry for her.
While New York is a great place, I wouldn't move there.
In fact, I will probably not visit again.
In other words, I was glad to say good-bye to Jenny.

ACTIVITY 6   Note the signal word and complete each sentence. Circle the letter of the correct answer.

1. She refused to quit in spite of her _____.
   a. illness
   b. success
   c. happiness

2. While I love living abroad, I _____.
   a. will move there soon
   b. speak many languages
   c. can't leave home now

---

* See Chapter 1 for use with internal definitions.

3. We won't be finished by _____.
   a. this evening
   b. now
   c. the office

4. Karla refused to marry Jack. In fact, _____.
   a. she never married anyone
   b. they got married two months later
   c. they are very happy

ACTIVITY 7 Work with a partner to complete each sentence. Make two predictions for each. Compare yours with another pair's.

1. The president made his speech despite _____
   _____.

2. Rain rarely falls in the Atacama Desert. In fact, _____
   _____.

3. Please don't open the door during _____
   _____.

4. While she never goes to the doctor, _____
   _____.

5. _____
   until they have done their homework.

Making Inferences

Inferences are "educated" or smart guesses. They are similar to ellipses. They are about information not directly stated. You may not know it, but you make inferences every day.

Understanding the Strategy

"Reading between the lines" is examining context. It is reading what **is** stated to figure out what **is not** stated in a text. Inferences are made about persons, places, things, situations, or ideas.

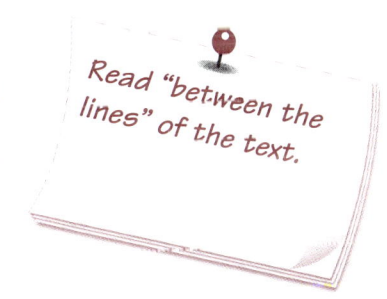

Read "between the lines" of the text.

152 CHAPTER 9

Example of inferring from a situation:

John is visiting Mary. He starts fanning himself with a piece of paper. He asks, "What's the temperature in here?"

Inferences:

1. John is hot.
2. John is nervous about visiting Mary.
3. John is hot and sick.

ACTIVITY. 8   Work with a partner. Read the paragraph. Make inferences about the situation.

The teacher called her name. Sylvia nervously went to the teacher's desk. Mrs. Marple didn't smile as she gave her the test. Sylvia looked at the grade quickly and then folded the test up. She didn't look at anyone as she returned to her desk. She sat down and quietly began to cry.

Inferences:

_____

_____

ACTIVITY. 9   Read each paragraph. Make inferences to answer the questions.

1. Puppies are popular Christmas presents. Sadly, many people do not understand that a puppy is a lot of work. These people get upset when their cute little puppy chews furniture, destroys carpeting, and eats shoes. They also get angry when they have to take the animal outside at inconvenient times.

    a. Is a puppy always a good Christmas present? _____

    b. Who should get a puppy? _____

2. The money wasn't bad, but the work was terrible. The students often laughed when I announced that their regular teacher was absent. No one listened to me. They refused to do their assignments. I sat and read while they talked. It was like we had an agreement. They wouldn't make trouble if I didn't make them work.

    a. What is the speaker's job? _____

    b. How does this person feel about the job? _____

3. Caroline decided to be a firefighter when she was ten years old. Her little brother almost died in a fire that year. A young firefighter saved him. The fireman went into the burning house and came out five minutes later carrying her brother in his arms. Caroline's family moved to a new town. For years, the townspeople laughed when she said that she planned to be a firefighter.

   a. What kind of person is Caroline? _____

   b. Why did people laugh at her? _____

   _____

Reading Difficult Material

The strategies in this book will help you read any text in English. Of course, some texts are extremely challenging. What do you when it is too difficult? The first rule is this: Don't stop. Keep reading!

Understanding the Strategy

Above all, you must keep reading. This allows you to follow the thread of ideas. Study the following tips for getting through difficult parts.

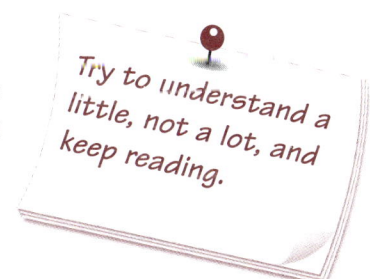

Try to understand a little, not a lot, and keep reading.

General Suggestions and Reminders

- Put a question mark in the margin and go on.
- Look for explanations of puzzling terms *later* in the text.
- Find main ideas stated in beginnings and endings.
- Remember that repeated terms will be important.
- Read the section many times; look for different information each time.
- Be patient: Try to understand a little, not a lot.

Special Tips for Rereading

When you read the section again, do the following:

1. Read slowly and carefully.
2. Break long sentences into small parts. Restate the parts in your own words.
3. Identify main subjects and verbs. Ask, "What did this . . . do?" and "Who or what did this?"
4. Pay special attention to signal words.
5. Try to separate main ideas from their supporting details.
6. Mark parts that are still confusing.
7. Go on. Keep reading!

ACTIVITY 10 Read the article, and try to understand what you can. Use the strategies for reading difficult material.

> When embarking on a diet to lose weight or improve health, many people first target fat for removal from meals. But nutritionists and dieticians say fat should not be dodged completely. In addition to making numerous foods taste better, fat is needed to help the body function properly, including storing energy.
>
> However, before you rush out for an order of french fries, learn the different types of fats and what they do for, or to, you. "In general, the beneficial fats are from plants, the harmful ones are from animals," says Karen Calabro, assistant professor of clinical nursing and coordinator for health promotion programs at the University of Texas School of Nursing at Houston. "Important exceptions are coconut oil and palm oil, fat from plants that are very high in saturated fat. In fact, higher than lard."
>
> The amount of fat and saturated fat is easy to determine on American food products that carry the nutrition label that is required on all but the smallest processed food packages. The FDA and USDA work together to set food labeling guidelines. Labeling is voluntary on raw fruits, vegetables, meats, and fish.

Remember

Outlining

Outlining organizes information. Like diagrams, good outlines help you remember and understand. They highlight key points and the relationships between them. Outlines are especially useful for difficult texts.

Understanding the Strategy

Outlines use a special form. The form shows the relationships between ideas and supporting details in a text. Letters, numbers, and indenting, or moving the text over, show if points are of equal, lesser, or greater importance.

Outline to remember and understand ideas and details.

How to Make an Outline

- Put the most important information or main ideas on the far left.
- Indent supporting details.
- Indent details/information of equal importance the same amount.
- Write in short phrases using abbreviations when possible.
- Use a letter or number system to separate main ideas from details.

Example

Main Idea: Development of Radio and Television

I. Radio
   A. Invention
      1. invented 1894—Marconi
      2. first radio signal 1901—Morse code
      3. first voice signal 1906—R. Fessenden
      4. first amplifier 1906—L. de Forest
   B. Growth
      1. existence of ionosphere proved 1924—E. Appleton
         a. reflects radio waves so can transmit around Earth
      2. microwaves introduced 1931
         a. shorter length reduces interference

II. Television
   A. Invention
      1. Nipkhow Disc 1884—for transmitting image
      2. cathode ray tube 1897
   B. Growth
      1. beginning of networks
      2. cable TV
      3. satellite TV

ACTIVITY 11 Write an outline for Reading 2 in Chapter 3 on page 47. Exchange your outline with a classmate. Read each other's outlines and explain if the relationships are correct. Correct your outlines if necessary.

PART 2: VOCABULARY STRATEGIES

Using Grouping and Classification

Internal definitions, grammar, word forms, and world knowledge all provide context clues to a word's meaning. Grouping and classification also provide context clues to a word's meaning. Identifying these grouping clues helps you figure out the meaning of unfamiliar terms.

Understanding the Strategy

Certain context clues indicate that a term is part of a group, or that it is naming a group or a class of items. Two clues for grouping are **"example" signal words** (for example, *such as*) that tell you examples are in the text and **lists.**

Look for grouping clues.

To use grouping clues to guess the meaning of unfamiliar terms, use the same method that you learned in Chapter 5.

Example of identifying an example signal word:

Citrus fruits **such as** oranges and pineapples are good sources of vitamin C.

What is *citrus fruits*?

- "such as" = signal word for examples
- oranges and pineapples = examples
- oranges and pineapples > belong to same *class*
- > *Citrus fruits* is a *group* of things or a *class* of fruit. (Yes, it is.)

Example of identifying a list:

Some of a farmer's most expensive equipment are tractors, harrows, and plows.

What is *harrows*?

- = 1 of 3 items listed
- list describes some of most expensive equipment
- equipment is class of things
- class of things used by farmer
- > *Harrows* is an example of farm equipment/tools, what a farmer uses. (Yes, it is.)

ACTIVITY 12 — Use grouping clues to guess the meaning of the underlined words.

1. The Empire State Building and the White House are two of the most famous edifices in the United States.

    edifices- _____

2. Kevin had no money or education, but these constraints didn't stop him from succeeding.

    constraints- _____

3. Diamonds, sapphires, rubies, emeralds, and other beautiful gems are in the necklace.

    sapphires- _____

4. Roses, tulips, and cleome are all growing in my garden.

    cleome- _____

5. They import commodities such as steel, rice, oil, and wheat.

    commodities- _____

6. We learned about squares, rectangles, circles, parallelograms, and trapezoids.

    parallelograms- _____

    trapezoids- _____

Using a Dictionary

You should not always use a dictionary as you read. However, a dictionary is necessary to learn. Dictionaries provide vital information in addition to definitions. Use your dictionary as a strategy for learning. Know the information it contains and how to find it.

Understanding the Strategy
A. Why use a dictionary?

Learn how to use a dictionary.

A dictionary provides vital information. You can:
- look up the exact meaning of a word.
- find out all of the meanings of a word.
- find out the part of speech of a word.
- find out the past tense of a verb.
- get the correct spelling.
- find out how to correctly divide the word at the end of a line.
- find out how to correctly pronounce the word.
- study examples of usage.
- learn formal and informal usages.

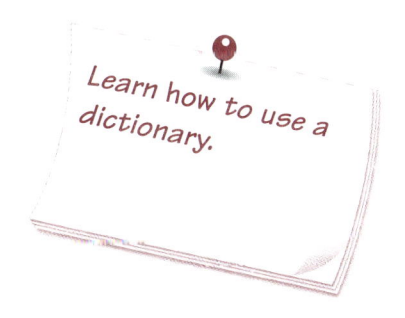

B. What is in a dictionary?

1. Types to choose from: Which dictionary is best?

An English-English dictionary has accurate definitions. Generally, it also gives more information. It usually has sample usage phrases or sentences for each entry, the grammar, and spelling rules. Many have indices of famous places and persons. *Unabridged dictionaries* list <u>all</u> English words. *Abridged* ones do not.

2. How to find words quickly

The words, or entries, in a dictionary are alphabetized. At the top of every page, *guide words* tell which words are listed on the page.

Example: guide words "overtake/ozone"

The words marked "X" will be listed on this page. The words marked "P" will be listed on a previous page. The words marked "N" will be listed on the next page.

- X overwork
- P overt
- X oxygen
- X own
- P overrate
- N ozone layer
- N ozonosphere

C. Reading a dictionary entry

Pronunciation

A dictionary tells how to pronounce a word. It uses a system with symbols you will need to learn. The system is usually explained in a guide in the beginning of the book. For each word, the pronunciation is between the symbols / and /.

    ground /ˈgraůnd/   flood /ˈfləd/   coin /ˈkȯin/

Dictionaries use different styles to show syllables and stress.

    pri-vate /ˈprī-vət/ (OR) /prī-vət/ (OR) /**prī**-vət/

Part of Speech

Always check the part of speech. Dictionaries generally use abbreviations such as "n." and "adj." to indicate parts of speech. Don't forget that many words such as *run* and *milk* can be more than one part of speech.

Meaning and Usage

Multiple meanings are numbered 1, 2, 3, and so on. The most common meaning is stated first. An example sentence or phrase using the word may follow. The example may help you understand the meaning even if the definition does not.

    For words with several meanings, you will have to decide which is correct for your reading. To do this, first check the part of speech. A noun meaning will not be correct if your unfamiliar term must be a verb. Next, test each meaning in the sentence from the reading and decide which makes the most sense.

ACTIVITY 13

1. Alphabetize the following group of words.
   bill   meaning   carport   soil   unmask   mask   beetle   lump   world

   _____

   _____

2. Alphabetize the following group of words.
   early   enemy   equator   egg   enclose   extra   extend   ear   eat

   _____

   _____

3. Alphabetize the following group of words.
   glide   glib   glaze   gloss   gloom   glad   glass   glance   glacier

   _____

   _____

ACTIVITY 14

Read the guide words. Put an "X" by words that will be listed on the page.

1. ligament / limitation

   _____ like   _____ line

   _____ library   _____ limit

   _____ lot   _____ light

2. flat / flippant

   _____ flavor   _____ flex

   _____ flap   _____ flock

   _____ filter   _____ fleece

3. cast / caterer

   _____ carry   _____ cause

   _____ coat   _____ cream

   _____ catch   _____ cat

ACTIVITY 15   Read each question and look up the underlined word in a dictionary. Then circle the letter of the correct answer.

1. Which of these would be a spontaneous event?
    a. Karen wins a tennis game.
    b. Dancing when you get good news.
    c. After planning for months, Larry asks Gina to marry him.

2. Which word is not a synonym of inspect?
    a. examine
    b. look for
    c. scrutinize

3. If you feel a situation is intolerable, you _____.
    a. are ignorant
    b. are not looking very hard
    c. are unhappy about it

4. What does prior mean?
    a. a person who lies
    b. happening before
    c. in a hurry

5. A transient situation _____.
    a. only lasts a short while
    b. is very dangerous
    c. happens over time

6. A hilarious story _____.
    a. makes people laugh
    b. is untrue
    c. is never funny

7. In order to improvise, you must _____.
    a. be a good carpenter
    b. think fast
    c. be strong and healthy

ACTIVITY 16

For each sentence, look up the underlined word in an English-English dictionary. Choose the correct meaning and write it in the blank.

1. The company <u>launched</u> a new sales plan.

   _____

2. This apartment is a <u>dump</u>.

   _____

3. He marched in and <u>stormed</u> about the house.

   _____

4. That asteroid follows an <u>eccentric</u> path.

   _____

5. The reporter got a big <u>scoop</u>.

   _____

Recognizing Abbreviations

Abbreviations are **shorthand.** They are a shortened, written form for words. You will often find them in applications and other forms, phone books, business texts, and measurements.

Understanding the Strategy

All abbreviations have few letters. Most end with a period (.). When an abbreviation is used with a proper noun, it begins with a capital letter. (Abbot Rd.). Study some of the following common types of abbreviations and examples of each.

Recognize abbreviations when you are reading.

Titles and Professions

Miss	unmarried woman
Mrs.	married woman
Ms.	married or unmarried woman
Mr.	married or unmarried man
Dr.	medical doctor or Ph.D. holder
Sgt.	sergeant
Prof.	professor
Atty.	attorney
M.D.	medical doctor (comes after a name: Diane Wilson, M.D.)
D.D.S.	Doctor of Dentistry

Addresses

Ave.	avenue	P.O.	post office
Apt.	apartment	P.O.B.	post office box
Bldg.	building	Cir.	circle
Dr.	drive	Blvd.	boulevard
Rd.	road	Hwy.	highway
St.	street		

Time

sec.	second
min.	minute
hr.	hour
P.M.	afternoon and evening
A.M.	morning

Days

Mon.	Monday	Fri.	Friday
Tue(s).	Tuesday	Sat.	Saturday
Wed.	Wednesday	Sun.	Sunday
Thurs.	Thursday		

Months

Jan.	January	Sept.	September
Feb.	February	Oct.	October
Mar.	March	Nov.	November
Apr.	April	Dec.	December
Aug.	August		

Measurements

c.	cup	lb.	pound
T.	tablespoon	ft.	foot
t.	teaspoon	in.	inch
oz.	ounce	sq. yd.	square yard
qt.	quart	sq. ft.	square foot

ACTIVITY 17

Rewrite each item. Spell out each abbreviation.

1. Dr. William Stanley, D.D.S. _____
2. Sun., Jan. 12, at 3:00 P.M. _____
3. 120 Apple Rd., P.O.B. 320 _____
4. Sgt. Julie McKenzie _____
5. Apt. B _____

ACTIVITY 18

Circle the abbreviations that do **not** belong to each group.

1. Addresses

   Hwy.   Apt.   Blvd.   Ms   Mon.   Cir.

2. Professions

   Dr.   Mr.   P.M.   Tu.   Rd.   Prof.

3. Titles

   Miss   Wed.   Thur.   Mar.   Apr.   Ms.

4. Time

   P.O.   hr.   min.   Mr.   sec.   Ave.   Sgt.

5. Months

   Bldg.   Nov.   M.D.   Oct.   Sat.   Dec.

6. Measurement

   sq.   yd.   ft.   hr.   c.   oz.   blvd.   lb.

ACTIVITY 19

Circle the terms that are not abbreviations.

Mr.   rd   min.   Go.   P.O.   t.   st.
Dr.   Sit.   Sat.   Apr.   T   dr.   Tu.

Reading: Along the Silk Road

Getting Started

Discuss these questions in pairs or small groups. Share your ideas with the class.

1. Have you heard of the Silk Road? Where is it? Why is it famous?
2. Why do you think it is called the Silk Road?

Strategies Reminder

Comprehension Strategies

Prepare
- Predicting from First and Last Paragraphs

Read
- Understanding Supporting Details
- Using Connectors (Ellipses) to Follow Ideas
- More Practice Using Signal Words to Predict Ideas
- Making Inferences
- Reading Difficult Material

Remember
- Outlining

Vocabulary Strategies
- Using Grouping and Classification
- Using a Dictionary
- Understanding Abbreviations

1 READING

Prepare

Work with a partner to answer these questions. Explain your answers to the class.

1. This reading is about _____.
   a. the Silk Road
   b. the name "Silk Road"
   c. the misnaming of the Silk Road

2. What is the main idea? Where did you find it?
3. Will there be terms about love in the text? Why or why not?
4. Think of a wh- question the text might answer.

Read

Read the text to get a general idea of the meaning. Don't try to figure out unfamiliar terms. As you read, think of the question you wrote in number 4 of the *Prepare* section. Mark key details as you read.

Journal of Asian-American Studies   May 2002

The Silk Road: Romantic but Misnamed

1   The name "Silk Road" is used by nearly everyone. And when we hear it, we can almost see the ancient caravans along the desert road, every camel carrying large bundles of the soft, beautiful cloth. But is our mental picture true? Perhaps not, and that is because the name itself is not.

A 19th-century German historian, Ferdinand von Richthofen, was the first person to use the name "Silk Road." However, the historian's term for this ancient route between China and Europe is not exactly correct. In fact, it is misleading. Why? There are two main reasons.

First, there is more than one route. China's trade routes to the West generally started at one of two places, Loyang or Changan. It is true that there was only one road leading west from these cities. From Changan, this route went up the Gansu Corridor and reached Dunhuang on the edge of the Taklimakan Desert. At Dunhuang, however, the route divided. Here, the road to the West separated into several branches.

Two of the branch routes were especially popular: the northern and southern. The northern route passed through Yumen Guan (Jiayuguan, or Jade Gate Pass) and then crossed the neck of the Gobi Desert to Hami (Kumul). Then it followed the Tianshan Mountains round the northern edge of the Taklimakan Desert. It passed through Turpan and Kuqa before it arrived at Kashgar, at the foot of the Pamir Mountains. The southern route branched off at Dunhuang, passed through the Yang Guan, and followed the southern edge of the desert, through Miran, Hetian (Khotan), and Shache (Yarkand). It finally turned north again to meet the other route at Kashgar. Many other smaller routes were also used.

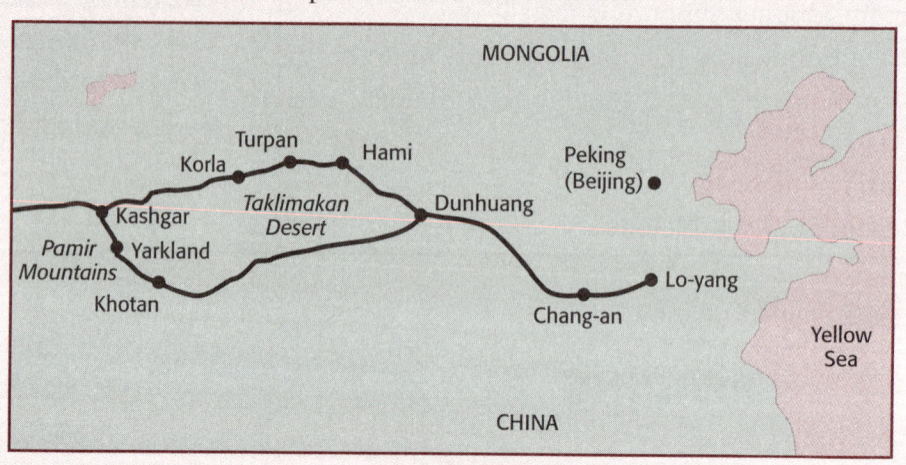

The Silk Road

Second, silk was not all that the caravans carried, although silk *was* the most remarkable commodity for the people of the West. Historians believe that the Romans first saw silk when they were fighting the Parthians in 53 B.C. The Parthians quickly realized that they could buy silk in the east and sell it to Rome. For this reason, the Romans saw this trade route to the East as a route for silk.

The name "Silk Road" is a misnomer especially because, in addition to silk, the route carried many other costly commodities. Caravans to China carried gold and other precious metals, ivory, precious stones, and glass. From China, traders also carried furs, ceramics, jade, bronze objects, lacquer, and iron. Traders did not usually travel the whole route, so goods were often traded several times. Traders bought goods in one place, traveled over part of the route, and sold them to another trader. For this reason, there are no records of Roman traders in Changan, or Chinese merchants in Rome.

Although the term "Silk Road" continues to be popular today, it is nonetheless misleading. It was indeed not one road but a network of routes. And while silk was an important commodity, it was certainly not the only one that traders carried.

Read Again

Read the text a second time. As you read,
- use the map to help you understand.
- mark difficult words and sections, but keep reading.
- identify the main idea of each paragraph. Restate it.
- try to figure out the meaning of important unknown terms.

Read the text a third time. As you read,

- use connectors and signal words to follow and predict ideas.
- check a dictionary for important words that you cannot guess.
- identify supporting details for each main idea. Evaluate them.
- think about the conclusion. Does it sum up the reading?

Post-Reading Activities

A. Comprehension Check

Answer these questions about the reading.

1. Find these places on the Silk Road map on page 166.
   a. Chang-an
   b. Taklimakan Desert
   c. Dunhuang
   d. Pamir Mountains
   e. Khotan

2. How did the Silk Road get its name? _____

3. Why is the name "Silk Road" romantic? _____

4. What were the most popular Silk Road routes? _____

5. In addition to silk, what goods did caravans carry? _____

B. Vocabulary Check

Work with a partner to answer these questions.

1. Read the passage. Identify the context clues to the meanings of the underlined words. Write each word next to the type of clue that best helped you determine the meaning.

   In addition to silk, the route carried many other costly <u>commodities</u>. Caravans to China carried gold and other precious metals, <u>ivory</u>, precious stones, and glass. From China, traders also carried <u>furs</u>, ceramics, jade, bronze objects, <u>lacquer</u>, and iron. Traders did not usually travel the whole route, so <u>goods</u> were often traded several times.

   a. grammar _____

   b. grouping _____

   c. internal definition _____

2. Figure out the meaning of each word.

Word	Prefix	Suffix	Part of Speech	Meaning
a. misnamed				
b. misnomer				
c. misleading				

3. Find and circle two synonyms for *expensive* in the reading.
4. Complete the chart for these words from the reading.

| Word | Do I know this word? | Is it important? | Is there an internal definition? | Other Clues |||
				Is it a noun? verb? adjective?	Does it look like a word I know?	Can I use world knowledge?
1. caravan						
2. bundle						
3. trade						
4. trader						
5. remarkable						
6. route						

What other words did you not know? If they are important to the main idea, list them here:

_____

5. Words used figuratively show the shape, size, or other feature of an object described in words. "Neck" is a part of the body. However, in the reading, it describes a place.

Example

neck > (narrow part of) desert

Write the <u>place</u> each of the following terms refers to.

    foot   corridor   branch

    a. foot   > _____

b. corridor > _____

   c. branch > _____

C. Following Ideas
Write the word or phrase omitted at the ▲ (ellipsis).

1. China's trade routes to the West generally started at one of two places, ▲ Loyang or ▲ Chang-an. _____
_____

2. The southern route branched off at Dunhuang, ▲ passed through the Yang Guan, and ▲ followed the southern edge of the desert, through Miran, Hetian, and Shache.
_____
_____

D. Predicting Ideas with Signal Words
Work with a partner to answer these questions. Share your answers with the class.

1. Scan the reading for signal words that are used in the following ways.

   a. addition _____

   b. balancing contrasting points _____

   c. emphasizing similar points _____

   d. time or sequence _____

2. Restate the ideas the signal words connect in your own words.

   a. _____

   b. _____

   c. _____

   d. _____

E. Identifying Main Ideas and Supporting Details

1. The main idea of this reading is: _____
_____

2. The two main supporting details are: _____

Remember

Complete the following outline.

The Silk Road

    I. Definition

    _____

    II. How it got its name

        A. _____

        B. _____

    III. Why the name is misleading

        A. _____

        B. _____

Discuss

1. Name other trade routes—local, national, or international. Tell the class about them.
2. Was trade important in the ancient world? Why or why not?

2. READING

Prepare

Work with a partner to answer these questions. Explain your answers to the class.

1. Who is Marco Polo? Skim the text to find out.
2. Think about Polo's adventures in China. Exchange ideas with another pair. Then prepare a list of important terms.
3. Will the reading say that Marco Polo did not go to China? Why?

Read

Read the text to get a general idea of the meaning. Don't try to figure out unfamiliar terms. As you read, think of the questions stated in number 3 of the Prepare section. Mark key details as you read.

The Adventures of Marco Polo—Fact or Fiction?

1 In 1260, Nicolo and Maffeo Polo, two businessmen from Venice, began a trip to China. At that time, there was little communication between China and Europe; there were thousands of miles of mountains and deserts between them. In fact, it took the Polo brothers five years to make the trip. Once there, the brothers met Emperor Kublai Khan, who was very interested in their stories of their home.

2 The Polo brothers returned to Venice in 1269. Two years later, they began a second journey to China. This time, they took Marco, Nicolo's 17-year-old son. This trip took three years. Along the way, they met Persians, Turks, Mongols, and people from many other cultures.

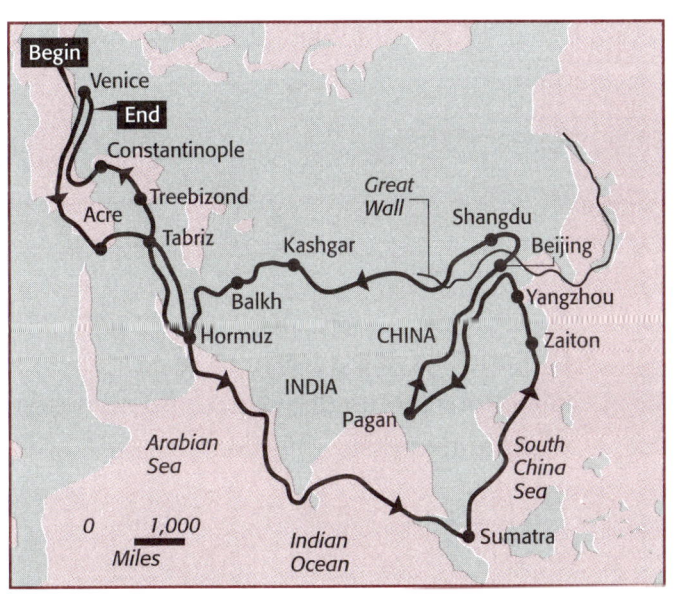

Marco Polo's path?
The route he said he took to China and back

3 Kublai Khan was happy to see the Venetians, and he gave them jobs. The Polos stayed at Kublai Khan's court. They worked for 17 years. By that time, Kublai Khan was almost 80 years old, and the Venetians thought that it was time to go home. A Mongol princess was leaving to marry a prince in Persia, so the Polos offered to go with her.

4 This time, the Venetian explorers went by ship. The three men sailed south with 600 people on 14 ships. The journey took four years. They finally reached Venice in 1295.

5 Soon after their arrival, Venice went to war with the city-state of Genoa. The Genoans captured Marco Polo and sent him to prison. There he met Rustichello, a popular writer of romance stories. Together, they created one of the most famous books in history, the *Description of the World,* also known as the *Adventures of Marco Polo.*

6 At that time, there were no printing presses, so copies of the book were made by hand. Despite this difficulty, it was soon the most popular book in Europe. Even Christopher Columbus studied it before beginning his journey in 1492. The book's popularity was especially surprising because it said that Chinese civilization was better than European civilization. According to Marco Polo, China was more civilized, far richer, and more advanced. People were especially amazed by Marco Polo's stories of the Emperor Kublai Khan. Marco Polo said that the emperor had 10,000 falconers and dog handlers and sometimes invited 40,000 guests to his parties.

7   Today, not everyone believes that Marco Polo visited China. Some say that he made up his stories with information from other people. They give several reasons for their disbelief. First, Marco Polo did not mention important aspects of Chinese culture such as the Great Wall of China, tea, or gunpowder. In addition, Kublai Khan's records do not mention Marco Polo or his father and uncle. As an old man, Marco was asked if he invented the stories. His answer may surprise you: "I told less than half of what I actually know," he said.

What other words did you not know? If they are important to the main idea, list them here:

_____

Read Again

Read the text a second time. As you read,

- use the illustration to help you understand.
- mark difficult words and sections, but keep reading.
- look for the reading's main idea. Restate it.
- try to figure out the meaning of important unknown terms.

Read the text a third time. As you read,

- use connectors and signal words to follow and predict ideas.
- check a dictionary for important words that you cannot guess.
- find details for each main idea. Evaluate them.
- think about the conclusion. Does it sum up the reading?

Post-Reading Activities

A. Comprehension Check

Answer these questions about the reading.

1. Write the date these events occurred:

   a. the Polos leave for China the first time   _____

   b. the Polos return to Venice the first time   _____

   c. the Polos leave for China the second time   _____

   d. the Polos arrive in China the second time   _____

   e. the Polos leave China the last time   _____

2. Why didn't people believe Marco Polo? _____

3. Where did Marco Polo meet Rustichello? _____

4. What was Rustichello's occupation? _____

B. Vocabulary Check

Work with a partner to answer these questions.

1. Find the related form of each word in the reading. Write it and identify its part of speech.

   a. *civilize* (v) _____

   b. *communicate* (v) _____

   c. *Venice* (n) _____

2. Underline three examples of foreign peoples that the Polos met. What is the phrase that groups these peoples? _____

3. Complete the chart for these words from the reading.

Word or Phrase	Do I know this word or phrase?	Is it important?	Is there an internal definition?	Other Clues		
				Is it a noun? verb? adjective?	Does it look like a word I know?	Can I use world knowledge?
1. journey						
2. arrival						
3. prison						
4. falconer						
5. made up						
6. Persia						
7. disbelief						

What other words did you not know? If they are important to the main idea, list them here:

_____

174 CHAPTER 10

C. Following Ideas

1. Write the word or phrase omitted at the ▲ (ellipsis).

    According to Marco Polo, China was more civilized ▲, ▲ far richer ▲, and ▲ more advanced ▲. _____

    _____

    _____

2. Write the word or phrase each item refers to. If the item does not refer to any word or phrase, put an "X" in the chart.

Word or Phrase	Line	Refers to
1. that time	4	
2. them	9	
3. there	11	
4. this time	18	
5. it	24	
6. her	25	
7. there	29	
8. it	35	
9. that	38	

D. Predicting Ideas with Signal Words

Complete the sentences with the correct signal word from the following list.

   despite   first   in fact   so

1. There were no printing presses, _____ copies of the book were made by hand.

2. There were thousands of miles between them. _____, it took the Polos five years to make the trip.

3. _____ this difficulty, it was soon the most popular book in Europe.

4. They give many reasons. _____, he did not mention gunpowder and the Great Wall.

E. Identifying Main Ideas and Supporting Details

Work with a partner to answer these questions.

1. This reading has two different parts. What is the topic of paragraphs 1–4? Of paragraphs 5–7?

   Paragraphs 1–4 _____

   Paragraphs 5–7 _____

2. What is the main idea of paragraph 7? _____

3. What details support the main idea of paragraph 7? _____

Remember

Draw a timeline illustrating the events of Marco Polo's life.

Discuss

1. Did Marco Polo travel to China? Why or why not?
2. Who are some famous explorers in your country? What did they explore?

3. READING

Prepare

Work with a partner to answer these questions. Explain your answers to the class.

1. Is this reading from an encyclopedia, a newspaper, or a magazine?
2. Will it be easy or difficult to read? Why?
3. Brainstorm *making silk*. Think about who makes it, and how it is made.
4. What is the most important question the text will answer? Write down your idea.

Read

Read the text to get a general idea of the meaning. Don't try to figure out unfamiliar terms. As you read, think of the question you wrote in number 4 of the *Prepare* section. Mark key details as you read.

SILK

History

Legend says that Chinese Empress Hsi Ling-Shi discovered silk in 2640 B.C. According to the story, she accidentally dropped a silkworm cocoon into a cup of tea. When she removed the cocoon, it unwound as a single thread. While this story may or may not be true, there is no doubt that the Chinese were the first to learn how to make silk. Remarkably, they were able to keep this discovery a secret for thousands of years. During this time, they made a great profit by selling silk to India, Europe, and the Middle East along the Silk Road.

Production

Silk is made from the cocoon of the silkworm. Silkworms have been raised in China and Japan for more than 4,000 years. *Sericulture*—the raising of silkworms—is still an important industry in parts of Asia, Europe, and the Middle East.

Silkworms eat leaves of the mulberry tree. After feeding for about five weeks, the silkworms stop eating and begin to make silk cocoons. A silkworm has glands that make a liquid that hardens into silk thread. The silkworm wraps itself in the thread by turning round and round. This movement forms the cocoon.

To remove the silk threads, factory workers put the cocoons into boiling water. This kills the larva and loosens the threads. Then the thread is carefully unwound. One cocoon may contain as much as 3,000 feet (900 m) of thread. Finally, several silk threads are wound together to make a thread large enough for weaving cloth. Therefore, it takes about 1,000 cocoons for one shirt and 3,000 to make one pound (454 g) of silk thread.

Silk threads are made into several fabrics such as chiffon, satin, and velvet. Silk is also used in ribbon, lace, and thread for sewing. Until nylon was invented, silk was used for women's stockings. In spite of synthetic fabrics, silk is still widely used because it is beautiful, light, and very strong.

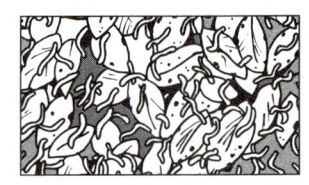

Silkworms eat leaves of the Mulberry tree.

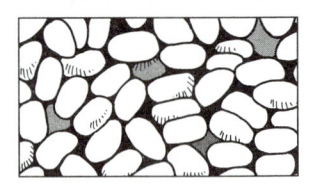

Silkworms wrap themselves forming cocoons.

The silk is carefully unwound after boiling.

The silk is spun together forming thread for weaving.

Read Again

Read the text a second time. As you read,

- use the illustrations to help you understand.
- mark difficult words and sections, but keep reading.
- find the main idea of each part. Restate the process in Part 2.
- try to figure out the meaning of important unknown terms.

Read the text a third time. As you read,

- use connectors and signal words to follow and predict ideas.
- check a dictionary for important words that you cannot guess.
- find details for each main idea. Evaluate them.

Post-Reading Activities

A. Comprehension Check

Number the steps of the silk-making process in order.

_____ Silkworms eat mulberry leaves.   _____ Silkworms make cocoons.

_____ Workers put the cocoons in hot water.   _____ Workers unwind the thread.

_____ The threads are woven into cloth.   _____ Silkworms wrap themselves in the thread.

B. Vocabulary Check

Work with a partner to complete the chart for these words from the reading.

Word	Do I know this word?	Is it important?	Is there an internal definition?	Other Clues: Is it a noun? verb? adjective?	Does it look like a word I know?	Can I use world knowledge?
1. legend						
2. accidentally						
3. cocoon						
4. unwound						
5. thread						
6. discovered						
7. discovery						
8. sericulture						
9. loosens						
10. weaving						
11. fabric						
12. synthetic						

What other words did you not know? If they are important to the main idea, list them here:

_____

178 CHAPTER 10

C. Following Ideas
Write the word or phrase omitted at the ▲ (ellipsis).

1. The silkworms stop eating and ▲ begin to make silk cocoons.

   _____

2. It takes about 1,000 cocoons for ▲ one shirt and 3,000 ▲ to make one pound (454 g) of silk thread. _____

   _____

D. Predicting Ideas with Signal Words
Complete the sentences with the correct signal words from the following list.

| also | despite | in other words |
| consequently | during | while |

1. _____ this may be correct, there is no doubt that the Chinese made silk first.

2. They made a great profit by selling silk _____ this time.

3. Silk is used for making satin. It is _____ used for making chiffon.

E. Identifying Main Ideas and Supporting Details
Identify the main idea of the reading. Is it stated in the first and last paragraphs? Why or why not? _____

_____

_____

Remember
How is silk made? Use a graphic organizer to show the process.

Discuss

1. Do you have many clothes made of silk? Why or why not?
2. What other kinds of material are clothes made from?

4 READING

Prepare

Work with a partner to answer these questions. Explain your answers to the class.

1. Is this a news article, a report, or a brochure? How do you know?
2. Which group of people is it written for?
3. Think about touring the Silk Road. What place names do you expect to see? List them in English if you can.
4. Think of a question. What will the text say about touring the Silk Road?

Read

Read the text to get a general idea of the meaning. Don't try to figure out unfamiliar terms. As you read, think of the question you wrote in number 4 of the *Prepare* section. Mark key details as you read.

Take a Silk Road Adventure!

Come with us on a romantic adventure tour! Our trip starts in Rawalpindi in northern Pakistan. From there we will travel on the famous Karakoram Highway built by the Chinese and the Pakistanis. This amazing road is the backbone of two incredible mountain ranges—the Himalayas and the Hindu Kush. These mountains have peaks that reach 7,000 to 8,000 m. They also include K2, the second-highest mountain on Earth.

On the Karakorum Highway, we will follow the River Indus to Gigit. Here, one feels the "real" mountains begin as the road climbs toward the Khunjerab Pass at 4,730 m. Then we will pass through the Hunza Valley, which is famous for its natural beauty, friendly people, and endless hiking and biking opportunities.

After we cross the world's highest international border, we will travel through ancient Silk Road cities such as Karakol, Tashkurgan, and Kashgar. We will also stop in Urumqi, at the foot of the Tianshan Mountains. This modern city is farther from the sea than any other city in the world. From Urumqi, we will go on to Turpan. It lies more than 500 feet below sea level and was once one of the most important stops on the Silk Road. From there, a short flight takes us to Dunhuang, the 2,000-year-old town on the edge of the desert. This is where the Silk Road divided into different routes. We will visit Dunhuang's famous sand dunes, where you will have a chance to ride on a camel. Finally we arrive in Xian—the eastern end of the Silk Road and the most popular tourist attraction in China. There you can visit the army of 6,000 life-size terracotta warriors that guard the tomb of China's first Emperor, Qin Shi Huangdi.

The Silk Road

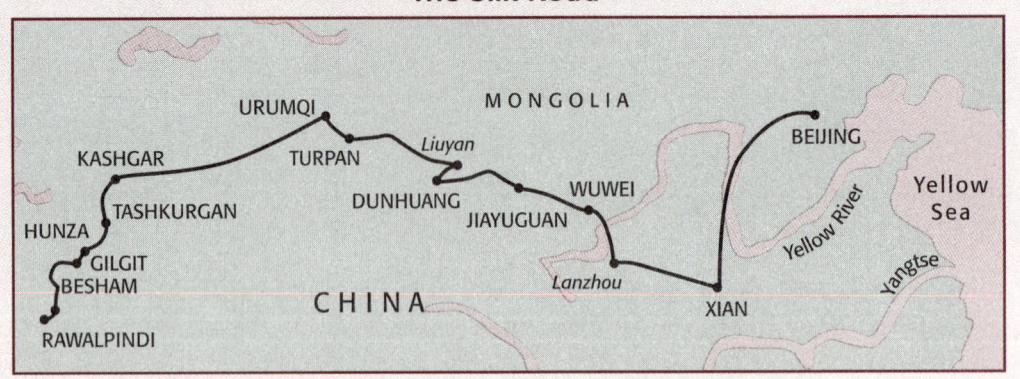

This fantastic opportunity is yours for $3,500.00.
The price includes airfare, meals, and hotels.
Contact us at www.adventuretour.com, or dial 1-555-SILK-ROAD.

Read Again

Read the text a second time. As you read,

- find each place on the map.
- mark difficult words and sections, but keep reading.
- look for the most important attractions of each place.
- try to figure out meaning of important unknown terms.

Read the text a third time. As you read,

- use connectors and signal words to follow and predict ideas.
- check a dictionary for important words that you cannot guess.

Post-Reading Activities

A. Comprehension Check

Complete the chart with information from the reading.

Place	Country	Important Information
1.		beginning of the tour
2. Himalayas		

Place	Country	Important Information
3.	between Pakistan and China	
4.		known for friendly people and beautiful scenery
5. Kashgar		
6.		farther from the sea than any other city
7. Turpan		
8.		where the silk road divided
9. Xian		

B. Vocabulary Check

Work with a partner to answer these questions. For questions 1–4, underline the correct answer in parentheses ( ).

1. A crossing high on a mountain is a (pass / pass through).
2. Caravans still (pass / pass through) the Pamir Mountains.
3. The Karakorum Highway is described as the (spine / the arms) of the mountain ranges.
4. *Terracotta* has (4 / 6) syllables.
5. Complete the chart for these words from the reading.

Word or Phrase	Do I know this word or phrase?	Is it important?	Is there an internal definition?	Other Clues		
				Is it a noun? verb? adjective?	Does it look like a word I know?	Can I use world knowledge?
1. incredible						
2. endless						
3. border						
4. flight						
5. divided						
6. sand dunes						

182 CHAPTER 10

Word or Phrase	Do I know this word or phrase?	Is it important?	Is there an internal definition?	Other Clues		
				Is it a noun? verb? adjective?	Does it look like a word I know?	Can I use world knowledge?
7. terracotta						
8. guard						
9. tomb						

What other words did you not know? If they are important to the main idea, list them here:

_____

C. Following Ideas

Write the word or phrase each item refers to. If the item does not refer to any word or phrase, put an "X" in the chart.

Word or Phrase	Line	Refers to
1. there	3	
2. this amazing road	5	
3. these mountains	7	
4. this modern city	21	
5. there	25	
6. we	28	

D. Predicting Ideas with Signal Words

Work with a partner to answer these questions. Share your answers with the class.

1. Scan the reading for these signal words and circle them.
    a. *after*
    b. *also*
    c. *finally*
    d. *then*

2. Find the ideas these signal words connect. Restate them in your own words.

   a. *after* _____

   b. *also* _____

   c. *finally* _____

   d. *then* _____

   ### E. Making Inferences

   Look at this passage from the reading. What is meant by "real" mountains?

   On the Karakorum Highway, we will follow the River Indus to Gigit. Here, one feels the "real" mountains begin as the road climbs toward the Khunjerab Pass at 4,730m.

   "Real" means _____.

Remember

Draw the route of the Silk Road Adventure Tour. Label it with important places and details.

Discuss

1. Is the Silk Road tour romantic? Why or why not? Would you go?
2. Would you like to be a travel writer? What do they do?

Reviewing Your Reading

A. Look at the following list of readings in this chapter. Check the column that shows how easy or difficult the material was for you.

Name of Reading	Easy	Average	Difficult
1. The Silk Road: Romantic but Misnamed			
2. The Adventures of Marco Polo—Fact or Fiction?			
3. SILK			
4. Take a Silk Road Adventure!			

184 CHAPTER 10

B. Read the following list of strategies that you have practiced in this chapter. Review the readings. Check which strategies you used, and how often you used them.

Strategy	Always	Often	Sometimes	Never
Prepare				
Predicting from first and last paragraphs				
Read/Read Again				
Understanding supporting details				
Using connectors (ellipses) to follow ideas				
Using signal words to predict ideas				
Making inferences				
Reading difficult material				
Remember				
Outlining				
Vocabulary Strategies				
Using grouping and classification				
Using a dictionary				
Understanding abbreviations				

C. Compare your chart with a partner's.

D. Did you use any other strategies while reading? If so, share them with the class. Explain where you learned them.

Reading: Hurray for Hollywood!

11

Getting Started

Discuss these questions in pairs or small groups. Share your ideas with the class.

1. What is Hollywood? Where is it?
2. Why is Hollywood famous?
3. What do tourists go to see there?

186 CHAPTER 11

Strategies Reminder

Comprehension Strategies

Prepare
- Predicting from First and Last Paragraphs

Read
- Understanding Supporting Details
- Using Connectors (Ellipses) to Follow Ideas
- More Practice Using Signal Words to Predict Ideas
- Making Inferences
- Reading Difficult Material

Remember
- Outlining

Vocabulary Strategies
- Using Grouping and Classification
- Using a Dictionary
- Understanding Abbreviations

1. READING

Prepare

Work with a partner to answer these questions. Explain your answers to the class.

1. What is the "sign of the stars"?
2. Make predictions about the main idea. Then predict the genre.
3. Brainstorm the "Hollywood" sign. Exchange ideas with another pair.
4. What will the text say about the famous Hollywood sign?

Read

Read the text to get a general idea of the meaning. Don't try to figure out unfamiliar terms. As you read, think about the question you wrote in number 4 of the *Prepare* section. Mark key details as you read.

TRAVEL MAGAZINE
For the Stay-at-Home Traveler

The Sign of the Stars: A History of a Famous Landmark

1   The Hollywood sign. One of the most famous landmarks in the world is now nearly impossible to see, but we can still learn about its interesting history.

2   The sign we see today is not the same one that the Hollywoodland Real Estate Company put up in 1923. At that time, the real estate company erected the original sign to advertise land in the Hollywood Hills. Each letter in the sign was 50 ft. tall and 30 ft. wide. The sign was lit by 4,000 light bulbs and was visible from 25 miles away. The company planned to keep the sign up for about 18 months. In fact, it lasted a lot longer than that.

3   The Hollywoodland sign became a symbol of the hopes and dreams of actors and actresses. However, the history of the Hollywoodland sign

shows that dreams do not always come true. In 1932, a young actress named Peg Entwhistle was sadly disappointed because she was not successful. Ms. Entwhistle hiked to the Hollywoodland sign. There, she found a ladder by the letter H. She climbed to the top and jumped to her death. Her suicide made people realize that Hollywood was also a land of broken dreams.

4   In 1944, Hollywoodland Real Estate Company went out of business. The owners gave the sign to the city of Los Angeles. However, no one was interested in it until the H fell over one day in 1949. At that point, the Hollywood Chamber of Commerce offered to fix the sign. They also decided to remove the last four letters.

5   This was not the end of the sign's troubles. By the early 1970s, it was clear that the sign needed more repairs. The Chamber of Commerce started raising money to rebuild it. Chamber of Commerce businesses "sold" letters to donors for $27,700 each. (Rock star Alice Cooper bought an O.)

6   Work on the sign began in August 1978 and was finished in November. The old sign was demolished, and new steel letters were put in its place. The sign is now 450 ft. wide but still 50 ft. tall. It weighs 450,000 lbs.

7   Every year, the sign of the stars attracts millions of tourists who want to see the sign in person. Unfortunately, many who come to see it never do. For example, some try to hike to the sign but get arrested. This is illegal, and the police fine them. Others try to drive into town. The view is good from the city streets, but the traffic jams are terrible. In other words, many tourists leave Hollywood only with a headache.

8   Now, however, there is one sure way to see the sign. Stay at home. Get comfortable at your desk and turn on your computer. You can visit the official Website (www.HollywoodSign.org) on the Internet. There, the world's most famous sign is now available for viewing 24 hours a day.

Read Again

Read the text a second time. As you read,

- mark difficult words and sections, but keep reading.
- identify the main idea of each paragraph. Restate it.
- try to figure out the meaning of important unknown terms.

Read the text a third time. As you read,

- use connectors and signal words to follow and predict ideas.
- check a dictionary for important words that you cannot guess.
- identify supporting details for each main idea. Evaluate them.

Post-Reading Activities

A. Comprehension Check

Mark each statement true (T) or false (F).

1. _____ The Hollywood sign was once a real estate advertisement.

2. _____ The sign we see today has been there since 1923.

3. _____ The Los Angeles Chamber of Commerce erected the original sign.

4. _____ A male actor named Entwhistle once jumped off the sign.

5. _____ In 1978, the city sold the sign for $27,700.

6. _____ The Hollywood sign today is much wider than the original sign.

7. _____ If you go to Hollywood, you can see the sign easily.

8. _____ Work on the sign began in November 1978.

B. Vocabulary Check

Work with a partner to answer these questions.

1. Find and circle a phrase that means "stop doing business."
2. Find and circle measurement abbreviations. What does each one stand for?
3. Find and circle a synonym for *not legal*. What is the prefix?
4. Find and circle three words beginning with "re". What part of speech are they?
5. Look up *demolished* in a dictionary. How is it pronounced?
6. Complete the chart for these words from the reading.

				Other Clues		
Word or Phrase	Do I know this word or phrase?	Is it important?	Is there an internal definition?	Is it a noun? verb? adjective? I know?	Does it look like a word	Can I use world knowledge?
1. landmark						
2. erected						
3. Chamber of Commerce						
4. repairs						
5. rebuild						
6. donors						
7. disappointed						

What other words did you not know? If they are important to the main idea, list them here:

_____

7. Find a class of tourists mentioned in the reading. List the two examples given.

   Class of tourist: _____

   Examples: _____

   _____

C. Following Ideas
Write the word or phrase each item refers to. If the item does not refer to any word or phrase, put an "X" in the chart.

Words	Line	Refers to
1. there	21	
2. that point	30	
3. this	33	

D. Predicting Ideas with Signal Words
1. Scan the reading for signal words that are used in the following ways.

   a. emphasizing similar points _____

   b. making a point clear _____

   c. time or sequence _____

2. Compare your answers with a classmate's.

E. Identifying Main Ideas and Supporting Details
Write the main idea and/or supporting details of each paragraph of the reading.

Paragraph	Main Idea	Supporting Details
1		
2		
3		
4		
5		
6		
7		
8		

Remember

Draw a timeline illustrating the history of the Hollywood sign.

Discuss

1. Name some other places that are a "land of dreams." Describe them.
2. If you visit Hollywood, what do you want to see? What other famous places would you visit?

2. READING

Prepare

Work with a partner to answer these questions. Explain your answers to the class.

1. What is the topic of this reading?
2. How is the information arranged? Why?
3. Brainstorm jobs listed on movies. What are movie "credits"?
4. Ask the text this question: What does a producer do?

Read

Read the text to get a general idea of the meaning. Don't try to figure out unfamiliar terms. As you read, think of the question stated in number 4 of the *Prepare* section. Mark key details as you read.

Glossary of Movie Credits

At the end of every movie are the credits. This is a list of the most important people who worked on the movie and their job description.

producer: The producer finds ideas for movies. He or she hires the director. Together, the producer and the director hire the actors. The producer also takes care of the money.

director: The director is in charge of making the film. He or she plans the camera shots and tells the actors what to do. A director usually has complete artistic control over the movie. The director also works with the producer to hire the actors.

cinematographer: The cinematographer is the director of photography. He or she is a person with a great deal of knowledge about the science and art of photography. The director has a mental image of what the film should look like, and the cinematographer tries to put that image on the screen.

art director: The art director is also called production designer. He or she designs the sets for a movie. This person needs to know a lot about architecture and interior design. He or she works with the cinematographer.

costume designer: The costume designer plans the clothes that the actors wear. He or she may create the clothes or buy them. The costume designer often has to do a lot of research to make realistic clothing for a particular time. The costume designer works with the director and the art director.

editor: When a director is making a movie, he or she usually has several different shots of the same scene. It is the editor's job to put different shots together. The editor works closely with the director.

camera operator: The camera operator takes the pictures. He or she follows the directions of the director and the cinematographer.

gaffer: The gaffer is the head electrician. He or she is responsible for lighting the set. The gaffer works closely with the cinematographer.

Read Again

Read the text a second time. As you read,

- think of two more questions and read to find the answers.
- mark difficult words and sections, but keep reading.
- restate each job description.
- try to figure out the meaning of important unknown terms.

Read the text a third time. As you read,

- check the dictionary for important words that you cannot guess.

Post-Reading Activities

A. Comprehension Check

Complete this diagram of the glossary. Write the name of the job or the responsibilities.

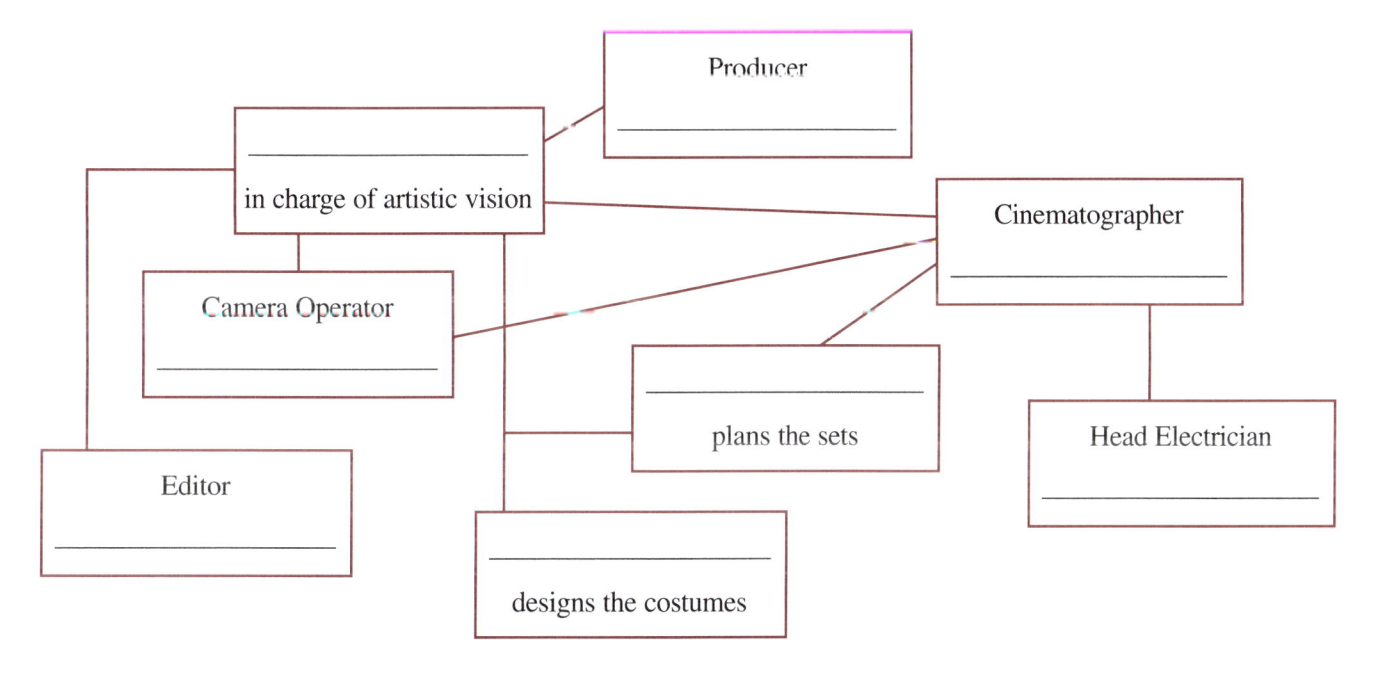

- Producer: _____
- _____ : in charge of artistic vision
- Cinematographer: _____
- Camera Operator: _____
- _____ : plans the sets
- Head Electrician: _____
- Editor: _____
- _____ : designs the costumes

B. Vocabulary Check

Work with a partner to answer these questions.

1. Find the related form of each word in the reading. Write it and identify its part of speech.

   a. *art* (n) _____

   b. *producer* (n) _____

   c. *real* (adj) _____

2. What suffix(es) do the job names have in common? Why?

3. Complete the chart for these words from the reading.

Word or Phrase	Do I know this word or phrase?	Is it important?	Is there an internal definition?	Is it a noun? verb? adjective?	Does it look like a word I know?	Can I use world knowledge?
1. credits						
2. in charge of						
3. mental						
4. image						
5. sets						
6. create						
7. research						

(Other Clues)

What other words did you not know? If they are important to the main idea, list them here:

_____

C. Making Inferences

Mark each inference true (T), false (F), or cannot say from the reading (X).

1. _____ The art director must understand the director's ideas.

2. _____ The cinematographer must know a lot about electricity.

3. _____ The producer knows a lot about lighting.

Remember

Change the diagram in Exercise A (*Comprehension Check*) to an outline. Be sure to indent and to use a letter or number system.

Discuss

1. Do you want a movie job? Explain your reasons.
2. What kind of movies do you like? Why?

3 · READING

Prepare

Work with a partner to answer these questions. Explain your answers to the class.

1. This reading is an interview. Which features tell you this?
2. What does Mary Zophres do?
3. How do you become a costume designer? List terms that might be in the text.

Read

Read the text to get a general idea of the meaning. Don't try to figure out unfamiliar terms. As you read, mark key details and look for the terms you listed in number 3 of the *Prepare* section.

Careerline
with JANICE JEFFRIES

This week our spotlight is on a job in movies and the theater—costume design. Mary Zophres is a costume designer in Hollywood. She has designed clothes for famous movie stars such as Leonardo di Caprio, Tom Hanks, George Clooney, and Catherine Zeta-Jones. She recently took time out of her busy schedule to talk with me about her life as a costume designer.

Janice: How did you get interested in costume design? Was it a lifelong dream?
Mary: I can't say that costume design was a lifelong dream. I've always been interested in clothes. When I was young, my parents owned a clothing store, and my first experience with clothing came from working in their shop when I was a teenager. I studied art in college, and one day I saw the film *Day for Night*, by French director François Truffaut. It's the story of the making of a movie. It was the first time I realized how complex and interesting moviemaking was. It looked like fun. That was when I started thinking about working in the film industry.
Janice: Is that when you went to Hollywood?
Mary: Oh, no. I couldn't go then. I didn't have any money or any contacts. And in Hollywood, contacts are important. You have to know people. After graduation from college, I got a job in the fashion industry in New York. I worked for several years and saved my money. Then I wrote to several people and offered to work for them for free.
Janice: You worked for free?
Mary: Oh, yes. No one pays you when you go to school, and I was no different than a student. I was very lucky. I got a job as an intern in an art department. I did that for a couple of years. My first break came when I got a job as a production assistant on *Born on the Fourth of July*. They paid me $200 a week. It wasn't much, but I was on my way.

Janice: So, what does it take to become a costume designer? Do you have to be a good seamstress?
Mary: Oh, no! Thank goodness you don't have to be a seamstress. I *can* sew, but not that well. Basically, I think that you have to have an eye for detail. There are differences in clothing styles that many people might not notice, but they make a difference.
Janice: Where do you get your ideas?
Mary: It depends. If the movie isn't contemporary, you have to do a lot of research to find out about clothes in that time. For example, *Catch Me If You Can* is set in the sixties. I got ideas from lots of places—old fashion magazines, of course, and even old high school yearbooks.
Janice: So, is your dream to win an Academy Award for Costume Design?
Mary: That would be nice, of course. But right now my dream is to work on what I call a "corset" movie—one where the women wear corsets and big dresses like they did 150 years ago. Designing those costumes would really be fun.

Read Again

Read the text a second time. As you read,

- mark difficult words and sections, but keep reading.
- note each question and answer. Restate them.
- try to figure out the meaning of important unknown terms.

Read the text a third time. As you read,

- use connectors and signal words to follow and predict ideas.
- check the dictionary for important words that you cannot guess.

Post-Reading Activities

A. Comprehension Check

Mark each statement true (T) or false (F).

1. _____ Mary Zophres first learned about clothing in her parents' store.

2. _____ Zophres studied costume design in college.

3. _____ After graduation from college, she worked in fashion design.

4. _____ For a while, she worked for free.

5. _____ She made a lot of money working on *Born on the Fourth of July*.

6. _____ Costume designers must be able to sew well.

7. _____ Details are important in costume design.

8. _____ Zophres does a lot of research for contemporary costumes.

9. _____ Zophres's dream is to win an Academy Award.

10. _____ Most women today do not wear corsets.

B. Vocabulary Check

Work with a partner to answer these questions.

1. Find and circle a phrase that means "to begin something."

2. List the words that make up each compound word. Then define the compound word.

   a. lifelong   >   _____ and _____ = _____

   b. moviemaking >   _____ and _____ = _____

   c. spotlight   >   _____ and _____ = _____

   d. yearbooks   >   _____ and _____ = _____

3. What syllable do you stress when you pronounce *corset*? _____

4. Complete the chart for these words from the reading.

Word or Phrase	Do I know this word or phrase?	Is it important?	Is there an internal definition?	Other Clues		
				Is it a noun? verb? adjective?	Does it look like a word I know?	Can I use world knowledge?
1. recently						
2. contacts						
3. intern						
4. break						
5. seamstress						
6. depends						
7. contemporary						
8. Academy Award						

What other words did you not know? If they are important to the main idea, list them here:

_____

196 CHAPTER 11

C. Following Ideas

1. Rewrite the following sentence with the information that is omitted (an ellipsis).
"I *can* sew but not that well."

_____

2. Write the word or phrase each item refers to. If the item does not refer to any word or phrase, put an "X" in the chart.

Word	Line	Refers to
1. it's	9	
2. it	9	
3. that	10	
4. that	24	
5. that	31	

D. Identifying Main Ideas and Supporting Details

List each question in the interview. Then list each question's main idea and the supporting details in Mary Zophres's answers.

	Question	Main Idea	Supporting Details
1.			
2.			
3.			
4.			
5.			
6.			

Remember

Outline reasons why someone you know should or should not design clothing for movies.

Discuss

1. How can a costume designer make a movie better or worse?
2. Describe some of the costumes for historical movies set in your country. Are they accurate? Why or why not?

4 READING

Prepare

Work with a partner to answer these questions. Explain your answers to the class.

1. What is Grauman's Chinese Theatre? Why is it a tradition?
2. Who will read this article? Where would you find it?
3. Brainstorm names of famous movie stars. Whose names will be in the text?
4. Ask the text this question: Why is Grauman's Chinese Theatre famous?

Read

Read the text to get a general idea of the meaning. Don't try to figure out unfamiliar terms. As you read, think of the question stated in number 4 of the *Prepare* section. Mark key details as you read.

Meet Me at the Red Pagoda
Grauman's Chinese Theatre—A Hollywood Tradition

Every movie lover who visits Hollywood should visit Grauman's Chinese Theatre. The theater looks like a giant red pagoda, and there is a huge dragon in the front. Inside there are exhibits of Chinese artifacts such as clothing, paintings, and weapons. However, don't be fooled—Grauman's Chinese Theatre isn't really Chinese. It wasn't built by a Chinese-American, and it doesn't show Chinese movies. What is the story behind this unusual place?

Sid Grauman opened the Chinese Theatre in 1927. He also built the nearby Egyptian Theatre. The first movie the Chinese Theatre showed was the premiere, or first showing, of the silent film *King of Kings*. Since then, the Chinese Theatre has had more movie premieres than any other theater. Because of a change in ownership, the theatre was known as Mann's Chinese Theatre from 1973 to 2000.

However, most people don't go to Grauman's Chinese Theatre to see a movie. They go to look at the sidewalk. There in the cement are the footprints, handprints, and autographs of more than 200 movie stars. These include stars from the past such as Marilyn Monroe, Elizabeth Taylor, Clark Gable, and John Wayne. But new stars are often added. In recent years, popular performers such as Meryl Streep, Whoopi Goldberg, Tom Hanks, Arnold Schwarzenegger, Harrison Ford, and Tom Cruise put their hands and feet in the wet cement. Directors Steven Spielberg and George Lucas and the *Star Wars* characters of Darth Vader, R2D2, and C-3PO did, too.

More than 2 million people a year visit Grauman's Chinese Theatre. Many of them compare their feet with the stars'. However, few are as small as Jeanette MacDonald's, a star of the 1920s and 30s. Her footprint is just 6 1/2 inches long!

In addition to the handprints, footprints, and signatures, you'll discover that some of the stars left other things:

- Comedian Groucho Marx left an imprint of his cigar.
- Cowboy actor Roy Rogers's horse Trigger left his hoofprints.
- 1940s movie star Betty Grable left an imprint of her famous legs.
- There are also cement impressions of two famous noses: Jimmy Durante's and Bob Hope's.
- And in 1995, Whoopi Goldberg cut off her braids and made an imprint of them in the wet cement!

Another amazing thing about Grauman's is the cost to tour it. The courtyard is free of charge to all visitors. You do not even have to buy a ticket at the theater to find the impressions of your favorite stars.

Read Again

Read the text a second time. As you read,

- use the photos to help you understand.
- mark difficult words and sections, but keep reading.
- identify the main idea of each paragraph. Restate it.
- try to figure out the meaning of important unknown terms.

Read the text a third time. As you read,

- use connectors and signal words to follow and predict ideas.
- check the dictionary for important words that you cannot guess.

Post-Reading Activities

A. Comprehension Check

Answer these questions about the reading.

1. Why is this theatre called Grauman's Chinese Theatre?
2. When did the theatre open?
3. Why is it famous?
4. How many tourists visit it every year?
5. What do many tourists like to do there?
6. What kinds of imprints can you find in the cement?

B. Vocabulary Check

Work with a partner to answer these questions.

1. How are the following words related? Try to define each one.

   a. footprint _____

   b. handprint _____

   c. hoofprint _____

   d. imprint _____

2. Complete the chart for these words from the reading.

Word	Do I know this word?	Is it important?	Is there an internal definition?	Other Clues		
				Is it a noun? verb? adjective?	Does it look like a word I know?	Can I use world knowledge?
1. pagoda						
2. dragon						
3. artifacts						
4. weapons						
5. fooled						
6. premiere						
7. cement						
8. autographs						
9. performers						
10. signatures						
11. impressions						

What other words did you not know? If they are important to the main idea, list them here:

_____

C. Following Ideas
Write the word or phrase omitted at the ▲ (ellipsis).

1. Inside ▲, there are exhibits of Chinese artifacts.
   _____

2. There in the cement are the ▲ of more than 200 movie stars.
   _____

D. Predicting Ideas with Signal Words
Use signal words to unscramble the sentences. Do not look at the reading. Rewrite the paragraph, putting the four sentences in the correct order.

However, few are as small as Jeanette MacDonald's, a star of the 1920s and 30s! In addition to the handprints, footprints, and signatures, you'll discover that some of the stars left other things. Many of them compare their feet with the stars'. More than two million people a year visit Grauman's Chinese Theatre. Her footprint is just 6 1/2 inches long.

_____
_____
_____
_____
_____

E. Identifying Main Ideas and Supporting Details
Write the main idea and supporting details of each paragraph.

Question	Main Idea	Supporting Details
1.		
2.		
3.		
4.		
5.		

Remember
Write an outline of the reading. Include all of the main points.

Discuss
1. Do you want to see the footprints of famous people? Why or why not?
2. Besides movie stars, what other famous people should leave their footprints for us?

Reviewing Your Reading

A. Look at the following list of readings in this chapter. Check the column that shows how easy or difficult the material was for you.

Name of Reading	Easy	Average	Difficult
1. The Sign of the Stars: A History of a Famous Landmark			
2. Glossary of Movie Credits			
3. Careerline			
4. Meet Me at the Red Pagoda			

B. Read the following list of strategies that you have practiced in this chapter. Review the readings. Check which strategies you used, and how often you used them.

Strategy	Always	Often	Sometimes	Never
Prepare				
Predicting from first and last paragraphs				
Read/Read Again				
Understanding supporting details				
Using connectors (ellipses) to follow ideas				
Using signal words to predict ideas				
Making inferences				
Reading difficult material				
Remember				
Outlining				
Vocabulary Strategies				
Using grouping and classification				
Using a dictionary				
Understanding abbreviations				

C. Compare your chart with a partner's.

D. Did you use any other strategies while reading? If so, share them with the class. Explain where you learned them.

Reading: Bridges

12

Getting Started

Discuss these questions in pairs or small groups. Share your ideas with the class.

1. Do you enjoy crossing bridges? Why or why not?
2. What are some bridges in your country? Describe one or two.
3. What will this chapter say about bridges?

Strategies Reminder

Comprehension Strategies

Prepare
- Predicting from First and Last Paragraphs

Read
- Understanding Supporting Details
- Using Connectors (Ellipses) to Follow Ideas
- More Practice Using Signal Words to Predict Ideas
- Making Inferences
- Reading Difficult Material

Remember
- Outlining

Vocabulary Strategies
- Using Grouping and Classification
- Using a Dictionary
- Understanding Abbreviations

1. READING

Prepare

Work with a partner to answer these questions. Explain your answers to the class.

1. What is the topic of this reading?
2. Describe the general style of this article. What genre is it?
3. Predict the main idea.
4. What is the most important question the text will answer?

Read

Read the text to get a general idea of the meaning. Don't try to figure out unfamiliar terms. As you read, think of the question you wrote in number 4 of the *Prepare* section. Mark key details as you read.

London Bridge Is a Tourist Attraction in Arizona

1   LAKE HAVASU CITY, Ariz.—People thought that Robert McCulloch was crazy when he decided to buy the London Bridge and move it to Arizona. First of all, the community that he wanted to put it in was only a few buildings next to a manmade lake. Second, how could anyone move a bridge around the world? Third, an English bridge would look ridiculous in the Arizona desert! But Robert McCulloch refused to listen. He wouldn't give up his dream.

2   In the early 1960s, the London Bridge was in trouble. Modern cars, trucks, and buses were too heavy, and the bridge was sinking into the Thames River. London officials wanted to build a new bridge, but they didn't know what to do with the old one. That was when McCulloch and a friend

offered to buy it. It cost them $2.4 million. At the time, it was the highest price ever paid for an antique.

3   Workers then began disassembling the bridge in London in 1968. They numbered the bricks before they put them on boats and sent them 10,000 miles to Los Angeles. At that point, they were put on trucks and taken to Arizona. Workers in the Arizona desert then reassembled the bricks according to a numbered diagram. Moving the bridge cost $7 million, but the bridge was finally ready in 1971.

4   However, McCulloch knew that he needed more than a famous bridge to attract people to Lake Havasu City, so he created an authentic English village next to the bridge. The village has typical English shops and pubs. Visitors can even ride on a double-decker bus and listen to the local radio station KBBC, known as BBC radio.

5   Today, the London Bridge is one of Arizona's biggest attractions, and Lake Havasu City is a lively town of 45,000—all because of the crazy dream of an Arizona businessman.

Read Again

Read the text a second time. As you read,

- mark difficult words and sections, but keep reading.
- identify the main idea of each paragraph. Restate it.
- try to figure out the meaning of important unknown terms.

Read the text a third time. As you read,

- use connectors and signal words to follow and predict ideas.
- check the dictionary for important words that you cannot guess.
- identify supporting details for each main idea. Evaluate them.

Post-Reading Activities

A. Comprehension Check

Answer these questions about the reading.

1. What does each number, date, or abbreviation refer to?

   a. $2.4 million _____

   b. 1968 _____

   c. KBBC _____

   d. $7 million _____

   e. 10,000 _____

   f. 1971 _____

   g. 45,000 _____

2. What was the "crazy dream of an Arizona businessman"?
3. Why did people think McCulloch was crazy?
4. Why did the British want to sell the London Bridge?
5. Why did workers number the bridge's bricks?

B. Vocabulary Check

Work with a partner to answer these questions.

1. What is the difference between *disassemble* and *reassemble*?
   _____

2. What is the meaning of the compound words *manmade* and *double-decker*?
   _____

3. Find and circle two abbreviations. Write their meanings here.
   _____

4. Complete the chart for these words from the reading.

Word	Do I know this word?	Is it important?	Is there an internal definition?	Other Clues		
				Is it a noun? verb? adjective?	Does it look like a word I know?	Can I use world knowledge?
1. crazy						
2. ridiculous						
3. sinking						
4. numbered						
5. bricks						
6. attract						
7. authentic						
8. typical						
9. pubs						
10. lively						

What other words did you not know? If they are important to the main idea, list them here:
_____

C. Following Ideas

Write the word or phrase each item refers to. If the item does not refer to any word or phrase, put an "X" in the chart.

Word or Phrase	Line	Refers to
1. that	16	
2. them	22	
3. that point	23	

D. Predicting Ideas with Signal Words

Find the main signal words in paragraph 1. List each one and state its purpose.

Signal Word   Purpose

_____   _____

_____   _____

_____   _____

E. Identifying Main Ideas and Supporting Details

Identify the main ideas and supporting details of each paragraph of the reading.

Paragraph 1: Main Idea _____

Supporting Details _____

_____

Paragraph 2: Main Idea _____

Supporting Details _____

_____

Paragraph 3: Main Idea _____

Supporting Details _____

_____

Paragraph 4: Main Idea _____

Supporting Details _____

_____

Paragraph 5: Main Idea _____

Supporting Details _____

_____

Remember

Outline the steps in moving the London Bridge to Arizona. Include key steps only.

Discuss

1. Should countries sell their important landmarks? Why or why not?
2. Would you like to visit Lake Havasu City? Why or why not?

2 · READING

Prepare

Work with a partner to answer these questions. Explain your answers to the class.

1. Where would you find a text like this?
2. Will the text be difficult to read?
3. Exchange ideas about bridges with another pair.
4. What will you learn about bridges? Ask the text two questions.

Read

Read the text to get a general idea of the meaning. Don't try to figure out unfamiliar terms. As you read, think of the questions you wrote in number 4 of the *Prepare* section. Mark key details as you read.

INTRODUCTION

Types of Bridges

There are three basic types of bridges: beam bridges, arch bridges, and suspension bridges. The biggest difference between the three is the distances they can cross in a single span. (A span is the distance between two bridge supports such as columns, towers or the wall of a canyon.)

For example, a modern beam bridge can span a distance of up to 200 feet (60 meters), while a modern arch bridge can span up to 800 or 1,000 feet (240 to 300 meters). A suspension bridge, the most sophisticated type of bridge, can span up to 7,000 feet (2,100 meters).

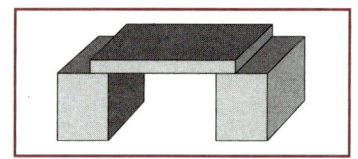

A beam bridge is the simplest design. It's very strong over short distances, but isn't strong enough for long ones.

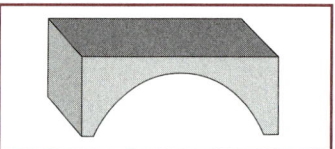

In an arch bridge, compression pushes the weight away from the arch and against the side walls and the material of the arch itself. The Romans were the first to build arch bridges. Some still stand today.

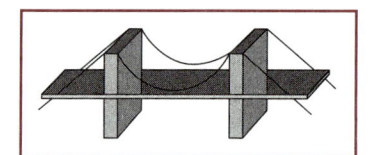

A suspension bridge hangs from cables at each end. Towers along the span also help support it. The cables are under tension. Suspension bridges are good for long distances.

Why can an arch bridge span greater distances than a beam bridge, or a suspension bridge seven times that of an arch bridge?

The answer is in two important forces, called **compression** and **tension**:
- Compression is a force that acts to compress or shorten the thing it is acting on.
- Tension is a force that acts to expand or lengthen the thing it is acting on.

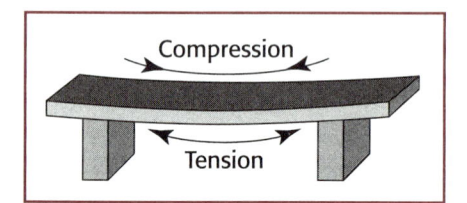

An ordinary spring is a good example of compression and tension. When we press down on a spring, we push the two ends of the spring together. In other words, we compress it. The force of compression shortens the spring. When we pull the two ends of the spring apart, we create tension in the spring. The force of tension lengthens the spring.

The forces of compression and tension are present in all bridges. The design of the bridge must be able to control these forces without buckling or snapping. When there is too much compression, a bridge buckles. When there is too much tension, it snaps. The best way to control these forces is to **dissipate** them or **transfer** them. To **dissipate** force is to spread it out. In this way, the force is not concentrated in one spot. An arch bridge is a good example of dissipation. To **transfer** force is to move it from an area of weakness to an area of strength. A suspension bridge is a good example of transference.

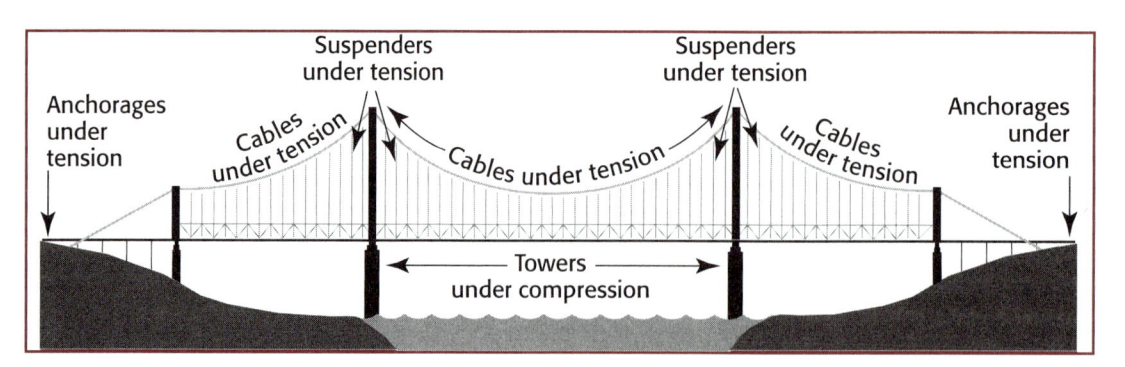

Read Again

Read the text a second time. As you read,

- use the illustrations to help you understand the text.
- mark difficult words and sections, but keep reading.
- mark main subjects and verbs of each section.
- try to figure out the meaning of important unknown terms.

Read the text a third time. As you read,

- use connectors and signal words to follow and predict ideas.
- check the dictionary for important words that you cannot guess.

Post-Reading Activities

A. Comprehension Check

Each statement in the chart describes a type of bridge. Check the column that applies.

Characteristic	Beam Bridge	Arch Bridge	Suspension Bridge
1. It can span long distances.			
2. It is the simplest bridge.			
3. It has cables and towers.			
4. It dissipates tension and compression.			
5. Romans built many of these.			

B. Vocabulary Check

Work with a partner to answer these questions.

1. Find the related form of each word in the reading. Write it and identify its part of speech.

   a. *compress* (v) _____

   b. *short* (adj) _____

   c. *length* (n) _____

   d. *dissipate* (v) _____

   e. *transfer* (v) _____

2. Complete the chart for these words from the reading.

Word	Do I know this word?	Is it important?	Is there an internal definition?	Is there an illustration?	Other Clues		
					Is it a noun? verb? adjective? I know?	Does it look like a word	Can I use world knowledge?
1. span							
2. support							
3. tension							
4. spring							
5. buckle							
6. snap							
7. concentrated							
8. weakness							

What other words did you not know? If they are important to the main idea, list them here:

_____

C. Following Ideas

Write the word or phrase omitted at the ▲ (ellipsis).

Why can an arch bridge span greater distances than a beam bridge ▲, or ▲ a suspension bridge ▲ seven times as much as an arch bridge ▲?

_____
_____
_____
_____

D. Predicting Ideas with Signal Words

Work with a partner to answer these questions.

1. Find each of these signal words in the reading and circle them.
   a. *for example*
   b. *in other words*
   c. *while*

2. Find the idea that came **after** each signal word. Restate it in your own words. Then, cover the reading. _____
   _____

3. Predict the idea that came **before** each signal word. Check the text to see if your guess is correct. _____
   _____

E. Identifying Main Ideas and Supporting Details

The text is divided into three sections. List the topic, main idea, and supporting details of each section in the following chart.

	Section Topic	Main Idea	Supporting Details
1.			
2.			
3.			

Remember

Describe an outline of the reading to the class. Explain the following items.
- which points would start on the far left
- which information would be indented
- the ordering system you would use

Discuss

1. What is the best kind of bridge for each place? Why?
   a. 4,000-foot span across an ocean bay
   b. a 120-foot span across a highway
   c. a 700-foot span across a deep canyon gorge

2. What are some famous bridges in other countries? Name the types if you can.

3 READING

Prepare

Look at the photo of the Akashi Kaikyo Bridge on page 202. Then work with a partner to answer these questions. Explain your answers to the class.

1. What is the purpose of this encyclopedia entry?
2. What method(s) will you use to read the text?
3. This article gives statistics about bridges. What terms do you expect to see?
4. Will the text explain why the Akashi Bridge was built?

Read

Read the text to get a general idea of the meaning. Don't try to figure out unfamiliar terms. As you read, think of the question stated in number 4 of the *Prepare* section. Mark key details as you read.

The Akashi Kaikyo Bridge: The Longest Suspension Bridge in the World

1. The Akashi Kaikyo Bridge is the longest suspension bridge in the world. It crosses the Akashi Straits from Maiko, Tarumi Ward in Kobe City to Matsuho, Awaji-cho, Tsuna-gun, on Awaji Island. The bridge took 20 years to plan and 10 years to build. It opened in April 1998. With a length of 1,911 meters, it is the longest suspension bridge in the world.

The 10 Longest Suspension Bridges in the World

Rank	Bridge Name	Length	Country	Year
1	Akashi Kaikyo Bridge	1,991 m	Japan	1998
2	Great Belt East Bridge	1,624 m	Denmark	1998
3	Humber Bridge	1,410 m	U.K.	1981
4	Jiangyin Bridge	1,385 m	China	1999
5	Tsing Ma Bridge	1,377 m	China	1997
6	Verrazano Narrows	1,298 m	USA	1964
7	Golden Gate Bridge	1,280 m	USA	1937
8	Hoga Kusten Bridge	1,210 m	Sweden	1997
9	Mackinac Bridge	1,158 m	USA	1957
10	Minami Bisan-Seto Bridge	1,100 m	Japan	1988

Facts about the Akashi Kaikyo Bridge

1. **Height of the main towers—about 300 m**
2. **Diameter of the main suspension cable—1,122 mm**
   Piano wire with a diameter of 5.23 mm was used to form the suspension cables. There are about 37,000 strands of wire in each cable. The total length of the cables is about 300,000 km.
3. **Size of the anchorage**
   The foundations for the anchorage sites on the Honshu end of the bridge have a diameter of 85 m and a depth of 63.5 m. About 350,000 tons of concrete were used in the anchorage.
4. **Strength**
   The bridge is designed to withstand winds blowing at 80 m/sec. The bridge columns can survive an earthquake of 8.5 on the Richter scale.

Read Again

Read the text a second time. As you read,

- mark difficult words and sections, but keep reading.
- note **types** of facts.
- try to figure out the meaning of important unknown terms.

Read the text a third time. As you read,

- use connectors and signal words to follow and predict ideas.
- think of more strategies to figure out important terms.

Post-Reading Activities

A. Comprehension Check

Scan the reading for answers to these questions.

1. What is the second longest suspension bridge in the world? _____

2. How old is the oldest of the ten bridges? _____

3. In what country is Hoga Kusten Bridge? _____

4. Circle which bridge is longer: the Golden Gate Bridge or the Great Belt East Bridge.

5. What kind of wire was used to form the cables of the Akashi Bridge? _____

6. How much concrete was used to anchor the Akaishi? _____

7. How severe an earthquake can the Akashi Kaikyo Bridge survive? _____

B. Vocabulary Check

Work with a partner to answer these questions.

1. Find the related form of each word in the reading. Write it and identify its part of speech.

   a. *long* (adj) _____

   b. *high* (adj) _____

   c. *deep* (adj) _____

2. Find and circle three abbreviations in the reading. Write their meanings here.

   _____

   _____

3. Complete the chart for these words from the reading.

Word	Do I know this word?	Is it important?	Is there an internal definition?	Other Clues		
				Is it a noun? verb? adjective?	Does it look like a word I know?	Can I use world knowledge?
1. diameter						
2. wire						
3. strands						
4. anchorage						
5. tons						
6. withstand						

What other words did you not know? If they are important to the main idea, list them here:

_____

C. Predicting Ideas with Signal Words

1. Identify the method that connects the text's main points.
2. List words you could substitute for the signal words. Compare lists with a classmate.

Remember

Make picture notes for the size of anchorage and strength of the Akashi Kaikyo Bridge. Compare your notes to a classmate's.

Discuss

1. How did people cross water before bridges were built?
2. What are the biggest dangers to bridges?

4 READING

Prepare

Work with a partner to answer these questions. Explain your answers to the class.

1. What is happening in the photos in the reading?
2. Predict the article's purpose and its main idea. When was this news story written?
3. Think about bridge disasters. What happens?
4. What will the text say about bridge disasters? About Galloping Gertie? Think of two wh- questions about the text.

Read

Read the text to get a general idea of the meaning. Don't try to figure out unfamiliar terms. As you read, think of the questions you wrote in number 4 of the *Prepare* section. Mark key details as you read.

The Collapse of Galloping Gertie

1 TACOMA, Wa.—Twenty years ago today, at 11:00 A.M., the Tacoma Narrows suspension bridge collapsed. The bridge, located near the city of Tacoma, Washington, was only a few months old. Even in that short time, the bridge had become known for its wild movements during high winds. Hence, its nickname "Galloping Gertie." On November 7, 1940, the bridge moved so violently that a support cable in the center of the bridge broke. This created an unbalanced load that caused the bridge to collapse.

2 According to design experts, there were several possible reasons for the bridge failure. Steel is commonly used to make bridges stronger. The weight of all the steel makes most bridges very stable, so engineers at that time didn't worry about wind. Due to a great increase of railroad and automobile traffic, many more bridges were built in 1940. However, because these bridges had lighter loads, engineers built much lighter bridges. The Tacoma Narrows Bridge was built using light steel.

3 This proved to be a tragic mistake. The winds in Puget Sound were strong enough to make the bridge move up and down a lot. However, this movement alone didn't destroy the bridge. In addition, a support bracket on the center span slipped and caused the center cables to loosen. This, in turn, caused violent twisting motions as the wind continued to blow and soon the bridge began to break up. Commuters plunged to their deaths in the cold waters of Puget Sound.

4 Architects and engineers remember the disaster. One expert said, "We didn't yet

understand the real importance of aerodynamics. After that terrible disaster, we had to find a way to predict how a bridge will behave in strong winds. We did it, using wind tunnel tests and mathematical models."

5 In 1950, a new $18 million bridge opened on the site of the first Tacoma Narrows Bridge. The four-lane deck has a design that resists torsional (twisting) forces. There are also special dampers at the ends to control movement.

Read Again

Read the text a second time. As you read,

- mark difficult words and sections, but keep reading.
- identify the main ideas. Restate them.
- underline main subjects and verbs of each section.
- try to figure out the meaning of important unknown terms.

Read the text a third time. As you read,

- use connectors and signal words to follow and predict ideas.
- identify supporting details for each main idea. Evaluate them.

Post-Reading Activities

A. Comprehension Check

Answer these questions about the reading.

1. How old was the Tacoma Narrows Bridge when it collapsed?
2. Why was the bridge famous?
3. What mistake did the engineers make?
4. When the wind blew, the bridge moved in two different ways. What were they?
5. What do engineers do today as a result of this disaster?
6. What controls movement on the newer Tacoma Narrows Bridge?

B. Vocabulary Check

Work with a partner to answer these questions. For 1–5, mark each sentence true (T) or false (F).

1. _____ *Galloping* is used figuratively. It compares the bridge to a horse.

2. _____ Gertie's *twisting* shows up and down movement only.

3. _____ A *suspension* bridge hangs from cables at each of its ends.

4. _____ *Steel* is a style of bridge.

5. _____ *Torsional* is a kind of force.

6. Complete the chart for these words from the reading.

Word	Do I know this word?	Is it important?	Is there an internal definition?	Is it a noun? verb? adjective?	Does it look like a word I know?	Can I use world knowledge?
				Other Clues		
1. collapse						
2. movement						
3. violently						
4. unbalanced						
5. stable						
6. bracket						
7. loosen						
8. wild						
9. dampers						
10. lighter						
11. aerodynamics						

What other words did you not know? If they are important to the main idea, list them here:

_____

C. Following Ideas

Write the word or phrase each item refers to. If the item does not refer to any word or phrase, put an "X" in the chart.

Word or Phrase	Line	Refers to
1. that	5	
2. this	10	
3. these bridges	19	
4. this	23	

218 CHAPTER 12

D. Predicting Ideas with Signal Words

1. Scan the reading for signal words that are used in the following ways.

   a. cause _____

   b. contrast _____

   c. effect _____

   d. time or sequence _____

2. In paragraphs 2 and 3, there are two "effect" signal words. List them here.

   _____ _____

3. Compare your answers with a classmate's.

E. Identifying Main Ideas and Supporting Details

Identify the main ideas and supporting details of the following paragraphs.

Paragraph 1   Main Idea _____

              Supporting Details _____

Paragraph 2   Main Idea _____

              Supporting Details _____

Paragraph 3   Main Idea _____

              Supporting Details _____

F. Making Inferences

Make two inferences from the following passage.

   Architects and engineers remember the disaster. One expert said, "We didn't yet understand the real importance of aerodynamics. After that terrible disaster, we had to find a way to predict how a bridge will behave in strong winds. We did it, using wind tunnel tests and mathematical models."

_____

_____

Remember

Use a graphic organizer to show the collapse of Gertie in your notebook.

Discuss

1. Have any bridges ever collapsed in your country? What do you know about these disasters?
2. When a bridge collapses should the engineers be blamed?

Reviewing Your Reading

A. Look at the following list of the readings in this chapter. Check the column that shows how easy or difficult the material was for you.

Name of Reading	Easy	Average	Difficult
1. London Bridge Is a Tourist Attraction in Arizona			
2. Types of Bridges			
3. The Akashi Kaikyo Bridge			
4. The Collapse of Galloping Gertie			

B. Read the following list of strategies that you have practiced in this chapter. Review the readings. Check which strategies you used, and how often you used them.

Strategy	Always	Often	Sometimes	Never
Prepare				
Predicting from first and last paragraphs				
Read/Read Again				
Understanding supporting details				
Using connectors (ellipses) to follow ideas				
Using signal words to predict ideas				
Making inferences				
Reading difficult material				
Remember				
Outlining				
Vocabulary Strategies				
Using grouping and classification				
Using a dictionary				
Understanding abbreviations				

C. Compare your chart with a partner's.

D. Did you use any other strategies while reading? If so, share them with the class. Explain where you learned them.

Appendix I

Scanning Practice

EXERCISE 1   Scan the television schedule. Find the following information.

1. What time is *Sports Desk* on?
2. What channel is *Mercy General Hospital* on?
3. What is the topic of *Eyewitness to History*?
4. What program would be good for gardeners?
5. What's on Channel 2 at 8:30?

Television

Tonight's shows	7:00	8:00	8:30
2 WGBH	**Newshour with Jim Thompson** (CC)	**Eyewitness to History** The story of Hurricane Andrew. (CC)	**All About Animals** The animals of Australia are featured. (CC)
4 WBZ	**Hollywood Squares** (CC)	**Entertainment Tonight** An interview with director Samuel Cox. (CC)	**King of Hearts** Jack loses his job but pretends that he got a promotion. (CC)
5 WCVB	**Inside Edition** A look at the steel industry. (CC)	**Chronicle** A visit to a tobacco farm in North Carolina. (CC)	
9 WMUR	**Entertainment Today** An interview with director Samuel Cox. (CC)	**Sports Desk**	**Bobby's House** Bobby decides he needs to get a second job. (CC)
11 WVTA	**Nightly Business Report** (CC)	**Antique Hunt** (CC)	
12 FOXNET	**Plants for all Seasons** Gregg shows the best plants for an indoor garden. (CC)	**LAPD: Life on the Street** Sam investigates the murder of a famous actor. (CC)	
13 WNNE	**Crosswords** (CC)	**Money Wheel** (CC)	**Who's a Millionaire?** (CC)

Tonight's shows	7:00	8:00	8:30
14 WNDS	News (CC)	Basketball The Kansas City Kings play the Seattle Triumph. (CC)	
15 UPN38	Mercy General Hospital Dr. Thorndike tries to save the life of a convicted killer. (CC)	Friends Forever Joe and Mike buy an expensive television, but they don't want their girlfriends to know. (CC)	What's Cooking? Dinah makes dishes from Japan and Thailand. (CC)
16 WEKW	Antique Hunt (CC)	Keeping Up with the Neighbors Martha wants to buy a new car. (CC)	Painting with Patty Patty demonstrates how to paint flowers. (CC)

EXERCISE 2

Scan the bus schedule. Find the following information.

1. What time does the first bus leave Woods Hole?
2. How many buses leave from Bourne on Sundays?
3. What time does the last bus arrive at Logan Airport?
4. How much is the fare from Falmouth to Logan Airport?
5. How many stops are there in Wareham?
6. What does "X7" mean?

Express Bus Schedule Woods Hole–Boston, Logan Airport
Combined Schedules effective January 1, 2004

	Leave Woods Hole	Leave Falmouth	Leave Otis Air Force Base	Leave Bourne	Leave Buzzards Bay	Leave Wareham Shore Road	Leave Wareham Mills Road	Arrive Boston	Arrive Logan Airport
X7	—	5:20	5:30	5:40	—	—	—	6:45	7:05
DAILY	—	6:10	6:20	—	—	—	6:30	7:30	7:50
X67 H	—	—	—	—	6:10	6:25	6:30	7:30	—
X7 H	6:45	7:00	7:10	7:20	—	—	—	8:25	—
DAILY	8:00	8:10	8:20	8:30	—	—	—	9:40	9:55
DAILY	10:30	10:40	10:50	11:00	—	—	—	12:05	12:25
DAILY	12:01	12:10	12:20	12:30	—	—	—	1:35	1:55
	2:30	2:40	2:50	3:00	—	—	3:10	4:05	4:25
X67 H	3:30	3:40	3:50	4:00	—	—	4:10	5:05	—
DAILY	5:00	5:10	5:20	—	5:45	6:00	—	7:30	7:50
7 H	6:00	—	—	—	—	—	—	7:25	—

Codes
Bold Face PM
6 Bus Operates on Saturday
7 Bus Operates on Sunday
H Bus Operates on Holidays
X Except Saturdays, Sundays, & Holidays (upon request to driver)

Fares
Woods Hole to Logan: one way—$22; round trip—$40
Falmouth to Logan: one way—$22; round trip—$40
Bourne to Logan: one way—$19; round—$34

For more information, please call 1-888-555-8800.

EXERCISE 3

Scan the course schedule. Find the following information.

1. What course does Professor Peake teach?
2. What time does Chinese 301 meet?
3. Where does Biology 202 meet?
4. What days of the week does Computer Science 134 meet?
5. What class meets in Clark Hall 204?
6. Who teaches Astronomy lab on Monday afternoon?

Course Schedule

Astronomy

Subject/CRN		Day	Time		Building	Instructor
ASTR-101-01	LEC	TH	0955AM	1110AM	Physics Bldg 203	Pasachoff
ASTR-101-02	LAB	T	0100PM	0230PM		Souza
ASTR-101-03	LAB	T	0230PM	0400PM		Souza
ASTR-111-01	LEC	TH	1120AM	1235PM	Physics Bldg 203	Kwitter
ASTR-111-02	LAB	M	0100PM	0400PM		Souza
ASTR-217-T1	TUT	F	0235PM	0350PM	Clark Hall 204	Cox

Biology

Subject/CRN		Day	Time		Building	Instructor
BIOL-101-A1	LEC	MWF	0900AM	0950AM	Sparkman Hall 112	Lynch, D.
BIOL-101-A2	LEC	MWF	1100AM	1150AM	Sparkman Hall 112	Lynch, D.
BIOL-134-01	LEC	MWF	1000AM	1050AM	Sparkman Hall 112	Edwards, J.
BIOL-202-01	LEC	MWF	1100AM	1150AM	Chemistry Bldg 123	Altschuler

Chemistry

Subject/CRN		Day	Time		Building	Instructor
CHEM-151-02	LAB	M	0100PM	0500PM		Skinner
CHEM-151-03	LAB	T	0100PM	0500PM		Skinner
CHEM-151-04	LAB	W	0100PM	0500PM		Lovett
CHEM-153-02	LAB	M	0100PM	0500PM		Bingemann
CHEM-153-03	LAB	T	0100PM	0500PM		Bingemann
CHEM-155-01	LEC	MWF	0800AM	0850AM	Chemistry Bldg 202	Peack
CHEM-251-01	LEC	MWF	1000AM	1050AM	Chemistry Bldg 123	Richardson, D.
CHEM-251-02	LAB	M	0100PM	0500PM		Richardson, D.

Chinese

Subject/CRN		Day	Time		Building	Instructor
CHIN-101-01	LEC	MTWHF	1100AM	1150AM	Stetson 308	Chang, C.
CHIN-101-02	LEC	MTWHF	1200PM	1250PM	Stetson 308	Chang, C.
CHIN-201-01	LEC	MTWHF	0900AM	0950AM	Stetson 308	Silber

CHIN-275-01	LEC	H	0700PM	0940PM	Stetson 308	Lu
CHIN-301-01	LEC	W	0110PM	0350PM	Stetson 308	Silber
		MWF	1000AM	1050AM	Stetson 308	

Computer Science

Subject/CRN		Day	Time		Building	Instructor
CSCI-105-01	LEC	TH	0955AM	1110AM	Chemistry Bldg 202	Murtagh
CSCI-105-02	LAB	H	0110PM	0225PM	Chemistry Bldg 217	Murtagh
CSCI-105-03	LAB	H	0235PM	0350PM	Chemistry Bldg 217	Murtagh
CSCI-134-01	LEC	MWF	0900AM	0950AM	Chemistry Bldg 206	Murtagh

EXERCISE 4 Scan the menu. Find the following information.

1. What kind of pancakes are served?
2. How much is a side order of bacon?
3. What is the most expensive omelette that is served?
4. How much would two eggs with ham, a small apple juice, and a side order of sausage cost?
5. How many kinds of eggs are offered?
6. How many pancakes are in a short stack? A tall stack?

Breakfast Menu

Eggs
Served with fried potatoes and toast

Two Eggs Any Style	$2.75
Plus your choice of bacon, ham, or sausage	4.50
Two Eggs Scrambled with Ham	4.50
Two Eggs Any Style with Two Pancakes	3.25
The 2-2-2	
2 eggs, 2 strips of bacon, and 2 pancakes (with French toast instead of pancakes, add 50¢)	4.00

Omelettes
Served with fried potatoes and toast

Plain	$4.25
Ham	4.50
Mushroom and Cheese	4.75
Ham and Cheese	4.75
Popeye's Delight *(spinach, tomato, and jack cheese)*	5.75
Vegetarian *(tofu omelette with onion, bell pepper, mushroom, avocado)*	5.95

Bread Choices
Whole wheat, rye, and white bread

Hot from the grill

Buttermilk Pancakes	
Tall Stack (4)	$3.25
Short Stack (2)	2.50
With bananas or berries, add 75¢	
French Toast	3.50
Belgian Waffles with Bananas	3.25

Breakfast side orders

Cream Cheese	.75
Fried Potatoes	$1.00
Toast	1.25
Sausage, Bacon, or Ham	1.50
Hot or Cold Cereal with Milk	1.85

Juices

	regular	large
Fresh Orange Juice	$1.50	$2.50
Fresh Grapefruit Juice	1.50	2.50
Apple Juice	1.25	1.95
Tomato Juice	1.25	1.95
Cranberry Juice	1.25	1.95

EXERCISE 5   Scan the chart. Find the following information.

1. How much does a room at the Pine Gardens Inn cost per night?
2. Does the Blain House have airport pick-up service?
3. Which hotels have kitchenettes?
4. Can you watch television at the Pine Gardens Inn?
5. Which hotels offer Internet access?
6. At which hotel can you go to a gym?

	Belvedere Hotel ($$$)	Blain House ($$)	Pine Gardens Inn ($$)
Hotel Facilities			
Restaurant	X		
Pool	X		X
Meeting Rooms		X	
Exercise Room	X		
Airport Pick-up Service	X	X	
Room Facilities			
Maid service	X	X	X
Kitchenette	X		X
Television	X	X	*
Hair dryer	X		X
Ironing board			X
Internet access	X	X	
In-room safe	X		**
Refrigerator	X	X	

Key
- $ $50–$75 a night
- $$ $80–$100 a night
- $$$ $110–$140 a night
- *   available in the lounge
- **   available at the front desk

Appendix II

Skimming Practice

READING 1

1. Skim the following article and choose the best title.
   a. Pioneer Life in the West
   b. Geography of the Great Plains
   c. The Plains Indians

2. In a continuation of this article, you would probably *not* expect to find information about _____.
   a. major cities in the Great Plains
   b. animals of the Great Plains
   c. Indians of the Great Plains

1   In the United States, tens of thousands of pioneers moved west in the mid-1800s. Some traveled to Texas. Others crossed the Rocky Mountains to reach California and Oregon. Still others settled in Utah. On their journeys westward, many of these early travelers crossed a huge region so barren that it is called the "Great American Desert." This region is the Great Plains.

5   Generally speaking, the Great Plains begin not far west of the Mississippi River and extend to the Rocky Mountains. On the north, the Great Plains stretch into Canada. On the south, they extend far into Texas. On the east, they merge with the prairies. In this huge Great Plains region, not much rain falls. It is a country of clear skies, where most of the land is flat, and the view ahead is straight and unbroken. Only in a few places are the flat plains broken by hilly or mountainous areas. The

10   most famous of these areas is the Black Hills in the states of South Dakota and Wyoming.

The early explorers and pioneers who traveled across the Great Plains found the land covered with grass. In most areas, this grass was shorter than the grass on the prairies. On the Great Plains, travelers saw few trees. Trees grew only beside streams or rivers. The most important river on the Great Plains is the Missouri River, a tributary of the Mississippi. The Missouri River is almost 2,500

15   miles long and has many tributaries of its own. These Missouri River tributaries include the Yellowstone River and the Platte River. Another river that crosses the Great Plains farther south is the Arkansas River.

The climate on the Plains can be extreme. The Great Plains are hot in summer. Then, the temperature often rises above 100 degrees Fahrenheit. In winter, especially in the north, the

20   temperature may fall to 40 degrees below zero. Winds sweep across the Plains since there are no mountains to break their force. When these winds blow in the winter, with the temperatures well below zero, the result is a freezing blizzard.

READING 2

1. Skim the following reading and say where it is probably from.
   a. a textbook called *The Business of Tourism*
   b. an article in *Vacationtime* magazine
   c. a newspaper article entitled "Largest Hotel in the World to be Built in Las Vegas"

2. In a continuation of this article, you would probably *not* expect to find information about _____.
   a. the best times to visit Las Vegas
   b. popular tourist destinations near Las Vegas
   c. water problems in Las Vegas

1   While other cities measure time in centuries, it seems Las Vegas sees history in weeks and months. Things happen quickly here, and if you turn away for a minute, you'll miss them. Indeed, if you haven't been to Las Vegas for a few years, you may not recognize it. Since 1992, the city and surrounding Clark County have grown by 320,000 people. A dozen huge hotels have opened along
5   the Strip. Fremont Street has become a downtown pedestrian mall. And the Chamber of Commerce is calling it the "Global Community of the 21st Century."
     If you've never been here, the sight can be overwhelming. Flying in at night, you see the valley's lights extend as far as the eye can see. The Strip, formally known as Las Vegas Boulevard, contains architecture that includes Roman forums, Egyptian pyramids, and New York City Gothic. In all, the
10   city has 13 of the world's 15 biggest hotels. The four hotels at Tropicana Avenue and The Strip—the Tropicana, Excalibur, MGM Grand, and New York-New York—have more rooms than all of San Francisco.
     Las Vegas is, first and foremost, a tourist town. Each year more than 30 million visitors fly or drive here. If they're typical, they leave slightly heavier after eating their share of bargain buffets.
15   And, with a few lucky exceptions, their wallets are quite a bit lighter. Tourists spend more than $22 billion annually, including $6 billion on bets.
     Nowadays, Las Vegas calls itself a "resort destination" where families can find a huge variety of restaurants, jump on thrill rides, and enjoy cosmopolitan surroundings. Old entertainers such as Liberace have been replaced by the Spice Girls. And while 1960s singer Wayne Newton still
20   performs here, he's not "Mr. Las Vegas" anymore. This city has grown up—it's not a one-horse (or one-singer) town anymore.

READING 3

1. Skim the following article and choose the best title.
   a. The Last Flight of Amelia Earhart
   b. Amelia Earhart: An American Hero
   c. Famous Women Pilots

2. In a continuation of this article, you would probably *not* expect to find information about _____.
   a. attempts to locate Earhart's plane
   b. other famous people who have disappeared
   c. how Earhart was honored after her death

Amelia Earhart was the most famous American female pilot who ever lived. She was born July 24, 1897, in Atchison, Kansas. In 1927, she became the first female pilot to complete a solo flight across the Atlantic Ocean. Four years later, Earhart attempted a flight around the world.

On June 1, 1937, Amelia and her navigator Fred Noonan left Miami, Florida. The first stop was San Juan, Puerto Rico. From there they flew along the northeast edge of South America and then on to Africa, the Red Sea, and Pakistan. They arrived in Calcutta on June 17 and from there, on to Rangoon, Bangkok, Singapore, and Bandoeng, Indonesia.

Monsoon weather stopped them from leaving Bandoeng for several days. During this time, Amelia was ill. It was June 27 before Amelia and Noonan were able to leave for Australia. At Darwin, the parachutes were packed and shipped home. Everyone agreed that they would be of no value over the Pacific.

Amelia and Fred reached Lae in New Guinea on June 29. At this point they had flown 22,000 miles, and there were just 7,000 more to go. Amelia sent a final newspaper article to the *Herald Tribune*. The photos show her looking very tired and ill during her time at Lae.

The U.S. Coast Guard ship *Itasca* had been waiting near Howland Island to act as a radio contact for Amelia because radio communications in the area were very poor. She left Lae at precisely 00:00 hours Greenwich Mean Time (GMT) on July 2. It is believed that the Electra had 1,000 gallons of fuel, enough for 20 to 21 hours of flying.

At 08:00 GMT, Amelia made her last radio contact with Lae. She reported being on course for Howland Island at 12,000 feet. There is no real evidence of the exact route of her plane. No one saw or heard the plane fly over. At 19:30 GMT, the following transmission was received from the Electra:

"KHAQQ calling Itasca. We must be on you but cannot see you . . .gas is running low . . ."

READING 4

1. Skim the following article. Where is it probably from?
   a. a journal article for weather forecasters
   b. a newspaper article warning of a thunderstorm
   c. a pamphlet on safety tips during severe weather

2. In a continuation of this article, you would probably *not* expect to find information about _____.
   a. how to figure out how far you are from a thunderstorm
   b. what to do in a snowstorm
   c. what to do if lightning strikes your house

Lightning is an underrated killer. In an average year, lightning kills and injures more people than hurricanes or tornadoes. For example, from 1990–1992, lightning killed 4 and injured 127 in Alabama. On the average, 80 deaths occur from lightning each year in the United States. Cars and homes are relatively safe from lightning. Playing golf isn't.

Lightning and the associated thunder can be frightening. But it doesn't need to be dangerous if you follow some simple rules. Stay inside buildings during a thunderstorm. Virtually all deaths from lightning occur outdoors.

If there are not any buildings nearby, cars and trucks (*but not golf carts or tractors*) can offer excellent protection. It is the outside metal surface, not the rubber tires, that offers the protection. Tires contain many other materials (*e.g. steel belts, etc. . . .*) that make them effective conductors, especially on wet roads. Golf carts and tractors do not have a metal surface surrounding the passengers, and therefore can be very dangerous. If you are caught in an open field, avoid isolated trees, hilltops, and metal objects (*e.g. golf clubs*). Also, stay out of water and get off small boats.

If your hair stands on end, your skin starts to tingle, or you hear clicking sounds, lightning may be about to strike. Get down on your hands and knees and keep your head tucked in. DO NOT lay flat on the ground. That can give lightning a better chance of striking you.

Thunder is the result of a lightning strike and cannot hurt you. Thunder is created when lightning heats up the air around it and causes it to expand rapidly. Because light travels very fast, you see lightning as it happens. Sound, on the other hand, travels much slower than light, and therefore takes much longer to get to you. So you hear the thunder after you see the lightning.